Mystical Magical Medicinal Mushrooms

A Comprehensive Guide to Cultivating Medicinal Mushrooms for Fun, Health and Profit

Jerrold D Puckett

To my dearest family and friends,

This book is dedicated to each and every one of you who has been an unwavering source of moral support throughout my writing process. Your belief in my abilities, your encouragement during moments of self-doubt, and your constant presence in my life have been instrumental in bringing this book to fruition. Your love and support have provided the foundation upon which my creativity and passion have flourished.

I would also like to extend a heartfelt dedication to Jeff Chilton, the esteemed co-author of "The Mushroom Cultivator," a book that has profoundly influenced my journey. Jeff, your collaborative work with the esteemed Paul Stamets has not only enlightened me about the intricate world of mushroom cultivation but has inspired me to embark on my own journey in this fascinating field. Your expertise, dedication, and unwavering commitment to spreading awareness have served as a guiding light, igniting my passion and deepening my appreciation for the natural wonders of the fungal kingdom.

To my family, you have been my unwavering pillars of support and love. Your belief in my dreams and your continuous encouragement have given me the strength to pursue my writing aspirations. I am forever grateful for the love, understanding, and encouragement you have showered upon me.

To my friends, you have been my constant companions throughout this writing process. Your friendship, laughter, and unwavering support have brought joy and inspiration to my life. Thank you for standing by me, offering your honest feedback, and reminding me of the power of genuine connections.

This dedication serves as a tribute to the profound impact each of you has had on my writing journey and my newfound passion for mushroom cultivation. Your unwavering support, love, and inspiration have propelled me forward, even during the most challenging moments.

With heartfelt gratitude and immeasurable love,

- Jerrold Puckett

Acknowledgements

I would like to extend my sincere appreciation and acknowledgment to the professionals at Amazon Publishing, who have played a crucial role in helping me publish my book. Their expertise and support have been invaluable throughout this process, and I am truly grateful for their dedication and commitment.

First and foremost, I would like to express my gratitude to the editorial team at Amazon Publishing. Their keen eye for detail, insightful feedback, and guidance have immensely shaped the final version of my book. Their expertise in editing and proofreading has ensured that the content is polished and ready for readers to enjoy.

I would also like to thank the design and formatting team for their exceptional work. They have skillfully crafted the cover design and layout, creating a visually appealing and professional product. Their attention to detail and creativity have truly brought my book to life.

Furthermore, I am grateful for the marketing and promotional support provided by the Amazon Publishing team. Their strategic insights and efforts in promoting my book have helped generate visibility and reach a wider audience. Their dedication to spreading the word about my work has been instrumental in its success.

Lastly, I would like to express my appreciation to the entire Amazon Publishing team for their professionalism, efficiency, and commitment to excellence. Their collective efforts have made the publishing process smooth and rewarding, allowing me to focus on writing and sharing my work with the world.

Once again, I extend my heartfelt thanks to all the professionals at Amazon Publishing who have contributed to the publishing of my new book. Your expertise, hard work, and support have been invaluable, and I am truly grateful for the opportunity to work with such a talented team.

Contents

Foreword

In recent years, people have become increasingly interested in the potential health benefits of medicinal mushrooms. These incredible fungi have been used in traditional medicine for centuries, and modern research confirms their powerful effects on both the body and mind. As a society, we are looking for natural ways to support our health and well-being, and medicinal mushrooms offer a promising avenue for achieving this goal. They have been found to boost the immune system, reduce inflammation, and improve cognitive function, among other benefits.

This book takes a deep dive into the fascinating world of medicinal mushrooms, exploring the scientific research behind their benefits and offering practical guidance on how to incorporate them into our daily lives. Whether you are new to the world of mushrooms or a seasoned enthusiast, there is much to discover within these pages. So come join me on this journey into the world of medicinal mushrooms and unlock the incredible healing potential of these powerful fungi.

CHAPTER ONE:

Why Grow Medicinal Mushrooms?

Mushrooms Species In this Book

Growing medicinal mushrooms can have a variety of benefits. Here are a few reasons why you might consider growing them:

- Health benefits: Many medicinal mushrooms have been shown to have various health benefits, such as boosting the immune system, reducing inflammation, and fighting cancer. Growing your own mushrooms gives you easy access to fresh, high-quality mushrooms that you know are free from pesticides and other contaminants.

- Cost savings: Medicinal mushrooms can be expensive to buy, especially if you're buying them in supplement form. By growing your own, you can not just save money but always have a steady supply of mushrooms on hand.

- Sustainability: Growing your own mushrooms is a sustainable practice that can reduce your environmental impact. Unlike traditional agriculture, mushroom cultivation doesn't require large amounts of water or land and can be done indoors or outdoors.

- Fun and educational: Growing medicinal mushrooms can be a fun and educational hobby. It can be fascinating to learn about the different types of mushrooms and their unique properties, and watching them grow can be a rewarding experience.

- Culinary uses: Many medicinal mushrooms, such as shiitake and lion's mane, are also delicious and can be used in a variety of culinary dishes. You can experiment with new recipes and add nutritious and flavorful ingredients to your meals.

The amount of money that can be made growing medicinal mushrooms can vary depending on various factors such as the type of mushroom, market demand, cultivation methods, production costs, and selling price.

Some popular medicinal mushrooms that are currently in high demand include Reishi, Shiitake, Cordyceps, and Lion's Mane.

The market for medicinal mushrooms has been steadily increasing due to the growing interest in natural and alternative health remedies. According to a report by Grand View Research, the global medicinal mushroom market size was valued at USD 24.85 billion in 2020 and is expected to grow at a compound annual growth rate (CAGR) of 9.5% from 2021 to 2028.

In terms of production costs, growing medicinal mushrooms can be relatively low-cost and can be done in small spaces. However, there are initial startup costs for equipment and materials, as well as ongoing costs for labor, substrate, and other supplies.

The selling price of medicinal mushrooms can vary depending on the type of mushroom, quality, and market demand. In general, medicinal mushrooms can sell for a higher price than culinary mushrooms.

Overall, the potential profit from growing medicinal mushrooms can be significant. Still, it depends on various factors, and it's important to do thorough market research and cost analysis before starting a business.

CHAPTER TWO:

The Lifecycle of a Mushroom

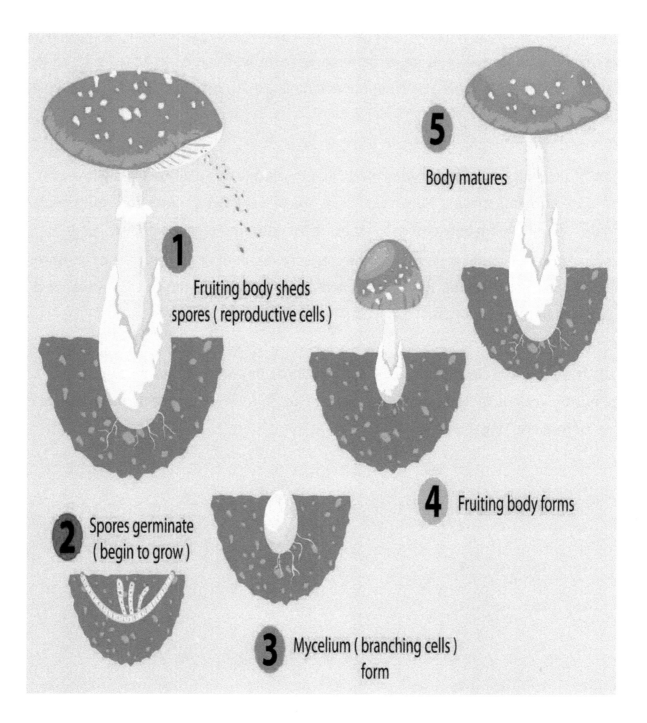

How to create mushroom extracts

The lifecycle of a mushroom consists of several stages, starting from spore germination and ending with the production of mature fruiting bodies.

Here are the basic stages:

1. Spore germination: The lifecycle begins with the germination of a mushroom spore. The spore is a tiny, microscopic structure that can be dispersed by the wind or other means.
2. Mycelium formation: Once the spore has germinated, it begins to grow into a network of thread-like structures called mycelium. The mycelium grows by consuming organic matter, such as dead plants or wood, and can spread over large areas.
3. Primordia formation: As the mycelium matures, it may develop into small, compact masses called primordia. These are the precursors to the fruiting body and can appear as small bumps or knots on the mycelium.
4. Fruiting body formation: The primordia continue to develop and grow into mature fruiting bodies, such as mushrooms or brackets. The fruiting body consists of a stem and a cap, and it is from this structure that spores are released into the environment.

Chapter Three:

Constructing A Sterile Mushroom Laboratory

Setting up a sterile mushroom laboratory can be a complex process, buthere are some general steps to get you started:

- Choose a clean, dedicated space: You'll need an area that can be kept clean and free of contaminants, such as a spare room or a garage. Thespace should be well-ventilated and free of drafts.

- Install necessary equipment: You'll need a laminar flow hood or a glove box to create a sterile work environment. You'll also need a pressure cooker or an autoclave to sterilize equipment and media, aswell as a digital scale, a pH meter, and other basic laboratory equipment.

- Obtain necessary supplies: You'll need sterile culture tubes, Petri dishes, agar media, sterile syringes, and other supplies for culturing and growing mushrooms. You can purchase these from a laboratorysupply company or a mushroom cultivation supplier.

- Develop and maintain sterile technique: Sterile technique is crucial for preventing contamination of your cultures. This involves wearinggloves, using a flame to sterilize equipment, and avoiding contact with non-sterile surfaces.

- Learn and follow protocols for mushroom cultivation: There are many protocols and techniques for growing different types of mushrooms. You can find these in books, online forums, or fromexperienced growers.

- Monitor and maintain laboratory conditions: You'll need to monitoryour laboratory's temperature, humidity, and airflow to ensure optimal growing conditions for your mushrooms.

It's important to note that setting up a sterile mushroom laboratory can be expensive and time-consuming. If you're new to mushroom cultivation, you may want to start with simpler methods, such as growing mushrooms from kits or using pre-made spawns.

CHAPTER FOUR:

Laminar Flow Hood for Sterile Work

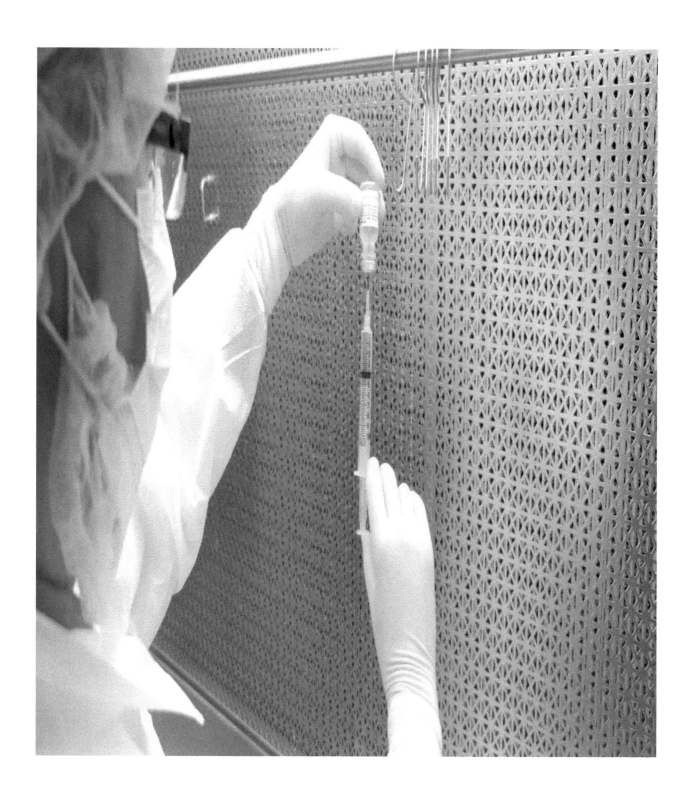

A laminar flow hood, also known as a laminar flow cabinet or clean bench, is a type of laboratory equipment used to create a sterile, dust-free work environment for the handling of sensitive materials.

The laminar flow hood works by creating a unidirectional, high-velocity airflow through a HEPA (High-Efficiency Particulate Air) filter. The HEPA filter removes particles from the air as it enters the cabinet, creating a clean, sterile working environment.

The laminar flow hood is commonly used in applications such as cell culture, microbiology, and electronics assembly, where contamination from dust or microorganisms could compromise the integrity of the work. The hood provides a protective barrier between the user and the materials being managed, and the laminar flow of air helps prevent contaminants from being introduced into the work area.

A laminar flow hood is an essential piece of equipment in sterile mushroom culture, as it provides a sterile environment for working with mushroom cultures and helps to prevent contamination. Here are some of the ways in which a laminar flow hood can be used in sterile mushroom culture:

- Sterilization of equipment: Before starting any work, it is important to sterilize all equipment that will come in contact with the mushroom cultures. This includes tools, containers, and media. Using a laminar flow hood, the equipment can be placed inside the hood and sterilized using heat or chemicals.

- Inoculation of mushroom cultures: Once the equipment is sterilized, the laminar flow hood can be used to inoculate the mushroom cultures. This involves transferring a small piece of mycelium (the vegetative part of the fungus) to a fresh substrate. The laminar flow hood helps to prevent contamination during this process.

- Transfer of mushroom cultures: As the mushroom cultures grow, they must be transferred to larger containers. The laminar flowhood can be used to transfer the cultures without introducing contaminants. This is done by placing the culture and the new substrate inside the hood and transferring the mycelium using sterilized tools.

- Harvesting of mushrooms: Once the mushrooms have grown, they need to be harvested. The laminar flow hood can be used to harvest the mushrooms without introducing contaminants. This is done by placing the mushrooms inside the hood and using sterilized tools to cut them off the substrate.

Overall, a laminar flow hood is an essential tool in sterile mushroomculture, as it helps to prevent contamination and maintain a sterile environment for working with mushroom cultures.

Chapter Five:

Mushroom Growing Chamber

Setting up a growth chamber for mushrooms involves creating a controlled environment that provides the ideal conditions for the growth and development of the mushrooms. Here are the basic steps for setting up a growth chamber for mushrooms:

1. Choose a suitable location: The growth chamber should be located in a clean, well-ventilated space that is free from drafts and temperature fluctuations. It should also be located near a power source.

2. Select a suitable container: The container used for the growth chamber should be large enough to accommodate the desired amount of substrate and mushrooms. It should also be able to maintain a consistent temperature and humidity level.

3. Install lighting: Mushrooms require specific lighting conditions to grow and develop. Depending on the species, they may require either natural or artificial light. Install lighting that provides the appropriate amount of light for the type of mushrooms you are growing.

4. Install heating and cooling systems: Mushrooms require a specific temperature range for growth and development. Install a heating and cooling system that maintains the temperature within the desired range.

5. Install a humidifier: Mushrooms require a high humidity level for optimal growth. Install a humidifier that can maintain the desired humidity level within the growth chamber.

6. Prepare the substrate: The substrate is the material on which the mushrooms will grow. It should be sterilized and inoculated with spores or spawn before being placed in the growth chamber.

7. Monitor and adjust conditions: Monitor the temperature, humidity, and lighting conditions within the growth chamber, and adjust as needed to ensure optimal growing conditions for the mushrooms.

It's important to note that setting up a growth chamber for mushrooms can be a complex process that requires careful planning and attention to detail. It's also important to follow specific protocols and techniques for growing different types of mushrooms, as different species may require different conditions and substrates.

What Type of Containers Can Be Used ForMushroom Cultivation?

Several types of containers can be used for mushroom cultivation, depending on the specific needs of the mushrooms beinggrown. Here are some of the most common container types used in mushroom cultivation:

1. Mason jars: Mason jars are a popular choice for growing small batches of mushrooms, such as oyster mushrooms or shiitake mushrooms. They are easy to sterilize and can be inoculated withspores or spawn.

2. Plastic bags: Plastic bags are often used for growing large quantitiesof mushrooms, such as button mushrooms or portobello mushrooms. The bags are filled with sterilized substrate and inoculated with spores or spawn before being sealed and incubated.

3. Plastic containers: Plastic containers are another option for growing mushrooms, especially if you want to grow mushrooms that require amore controlled environment. They can be used to grow mushroomssuch as lion's mane, enoki, or king oyster mushrooms. These containers are filled with sterilized substrate and inoculated with spawn, then sealed and placed in a growth chamber.

4. Wooden logs: Wooden logs can be used to grow certain types of mushrooms, such as shiitake or oyster mushrooms. The logs are inoculated with spores or spawn and incubated until the mycelium colonizes the log. Once colonized, the logs can be placed in a humidenvironment, and the mushrooms will begin to grow.

5. Grow bags: Grow bags are a convenient option for growing mushrooms, as they are pre-sterilized and ready to use. They areoften used for growing gourmet mushrooms such as shiitake or oyster mushrooms.

It's important to note that the container used for mushroom cultivation should be clean and sterilized before use to prevent contamination by unwanted microorganisms. Additionally, different mushroom species havedifferent growing requirements and may require specific containers and growing methods.

CHAPTER SIX:

How to Make a Spore Print

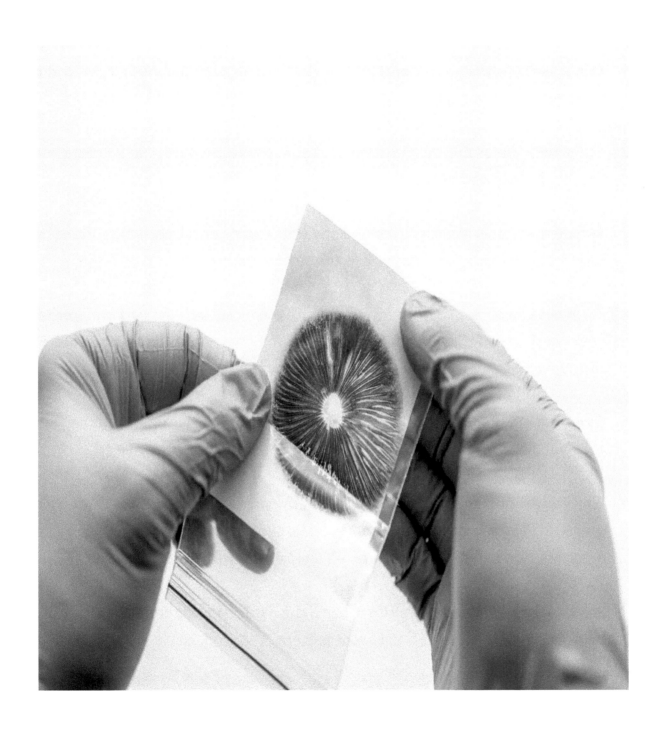

Making a mushroom spore print is a simple process that involves collecting spores from a mature mushroom and imprinting them onto a piece of paper or foil. Here are the basic steps for making a mushroom spore print:

1. Select a mature mushroom: Choose a mushroom that is fully mature and has an open cap. Make sure the gills or pores underneath the cap are fully developed and have turned dark in color.

2. Cut off the stem: Cut off the stem of the mushroom, leaving the cap attached to the rest of the fruiting body.

3. Prepare a surface: Place a piece of clean white paper or foil on a flat surface. Make sure the surface is clean and free from any contaminants.

4. Place the cap on the surface: Place the mushroom cap with the gills or pores facing downwards onto the surface of the paper or foil. Make sure the cap is centered on the paper or foil.

5. Cover the mushroom: Cover the mushroom with a bowl or jar to prevent any airflow that could disturb the spores.

6. Wait for the spores to drop: Leave the mushroom undisturbed for several hours or overnight. The spores will drop from the gills or pores onto the paper or foil, forming a pattern that reflects the mushroom's unique characteristics.

7. Remove the mushroom: Carefully remove the mushroom cap from the paper or foil, being careful not to disturb the spore pattern.

8. Store the spore print: Allow the spore print to dry completely, then store it in a dry, cool place until you're ready to use it.

Mushroom spore prints can be used to grow new mushrooms from the collected spores. However, it's important to note that different mushroom species may require different growing methods and substrates. Hence, it's important to research the specific requirements for the species you're interested in growing. Additionally, spore prints should be handled with care to prevent contamination and should be stored in a clean, dry environment to maintain.

CHAPTER SEVEN:

Sterile Agar Technique For Mushroom Cultivation

To make sterile agar for mushroom cultivation, you will need the following materials and equipment:

- Agar powder
- Nutrient source (such as potato dextrose or malt extract)
- Distilled water
- Autoclave or pressure cooker
- Laminar flow hood or glove box
- Sterilized glass containers (such as Petri dishes or culture tubes)
- Alcohol burner or propane torch
- Sterilized utensils (such as a spatula or pipette)

Here are the steps to make sterile agar for mushroom cultivation:

1. Prepare the nutrient solution: Follow the instructions on the nutrient source to prepare the solution. This typically involves mixing the nutrient source with distilled water and heating it until the ingredients are fully dissolved.

2. Add the agar: Weigh out the appropriate amount of agar powder and add it to the nutrient solution. Stir the mixture until the agar is fully dissolved.

3. Sterilize the agar: Pour the agar mixture into sterilized glass containers, such as Petri dishes or culture tubes. Place the containers in an autoclave or pressure cooker and sterilize them at 15 psi for at least 15 minutes.

4. Cool the agar: Once the agar is sterilized, allow it to cool to room temperature. This can be done in a laminar flow hood or glove box to maintain sterility.

5. Inoculate the agar: Use sterilized utensils, such as a spatula or pipette, to inoculate the cooled agar with the desired mushroom spores or mycelium. This should also be done in a laminar flow hood or glove box to maintain sterility.

6. Incubate the agar: Once the agar has been inoculated, seal the containers with sterile tape and incubate them in a controlled environment at the appropriate temperature and humidity for the specific mushroom species being cultivated.

It's important to note that sterile technique is critical when making agar for mushroom cultivation, as any contamination can lead to the growth of unwanted microorganisms and the failure of the mushroom culture.

Therefore, it's recommended to work in a clean, controlled environment, such as a laminar flow hood or glove box, and to sterilize all materials and equipment before use.

Here is a recipe for malt extract agar for mushroom cultivation:

Ingredients:

- 20 g malt extract
- 20 g agar
- 1 L distilled water

Instructions:

1. Dissolve 20 g of malt extract and 20 g of agar in 1 L of distilled water.
2. Mix the solution well and heat it until it boils.
3. Stir the solution continuously while boiling for about 2-3 minutes to ensure that the malt extract and agar are fully dissolved.
4. Once the solution is fully dissolved, turn off the heat and allow it to cool to about 50-60°C (122-140°F).
5. Pour the agar mixture into sterilized Petri dishes or culture tubes, leaving enough headspace to allow for expansion.
6. Seal the dishes or tubes with sterile tape and allow them to cool and solidify at room temperature.
7. The agar plates or tubes are now ready to be sterilized before inoculation with mushroom cultures.

Note: This recipe is just one example of many different agar formulations that can be used for mushroom cultivation. Depending on the specific needs of the mushroom species being cultivated, different nutrient sources or additives may be used to optimize growth and development. It's important to thoroughly research and understand the specific requirements of the mushroom species being cultivated to choose the appropriate agar recipe. Additionally, sterile technique is crucial throughout the entire process to prevent contamination and ensure successful growth of the mushroom cultures.

Here is a recipe for potato dextrose agar (PDA) for mushroom cultivation:

Ingredients:
- 200 g diced potatoes
- 20 g dextrose
- 15 g agar
- 1 L distilled water

Instructions:

1. Clean and peel 200 g of potatoes, cut them into small pieces, and boil them in 1 L of distilled water for 30 minutes.
2. Strain the potato water through a fine sieve or cheesecloth to remove any solid particles.
3. Add 20 g of dextrose and 15 g of agar to the potato water and stir the mixture until the ingredients are fully dissolved.
4. Heat the mixture while stirring continuously until it comes to a boil. 5. Boil the mixture for 1-2 minutes to ensure that the agar is fully dissolved.
5. Once the mixture is fully dissolved, turn off the heat and allow it to cool to about 50-60°C (122-140°F).
6. Pour the agar mixture into sterilized Petri dishes or culture tubes, leaving enough

headspace to allow for expansion.

7. Seal the dishes or tubes with sterile tape and allow them to cool and solidify at room temperature.

The agar plates or tubes are now ready to be sterilized before inoculation with mushroom cultures.

Note: This recipe is just one example of many different agar formulations that can be used for mushroom cultivation. Depending on the specific needs of the mushroom species being cultivated, different nutrient sources or additives may be used to optimize growth and development. It's important to thoroughly research and understand the specific requirements of the mushroom species being cultivated to choose the appropriate agar recipe. Additionally, sterile technique is crucial throughout the entire process to prevent contamination and ensure successful growth of the mushroom cultures.

Sterility is incredibly important in sterile agar culture for several reasons:

1. Preventing contamination: Sterility is essential to prevent the growth of unwanted microorganisms, such as bacteria and fungi, in the agar culture. These contaminants can compete with the mushroom mycelium for nutrients, overgrow the culture, and render it unusable for further cultivation.

2. Ensuring purity: Sterility also helps ensure that the culture remains pure, meaning it contains only the desired mushroom species or strain. Any contamination can lead to genetic drift, making it difficult to reproduce consistent results or maintain the original characteristics of the culture.

3. Facilitating growth: Mushrooms are sensitive organisms that require specific nutrients and environmental conditions to grow properly. Sterile conditions help ensure that the agar culture provides a clean and optimal growth medium for the mycelium to grow, allowing for healthy and robust mushroom production.

Overall, sterility is crucial for successful mushroom cultivation, as it helps prevent contamination, maintain purity, and facilitate healthy growth of the mycelium.

Chapter Eight:

Liquid Culture of Mushrooms

Here are the general steps to make a mushroom spore syringe:

Materials:

- Mature mushroom cap with gills or pores
- Sterile water or sterile saline solution
- Alcohol (70% isopropyl or ethanol)
- Syringe (10-20 mL)
- Sterile needle (18-20 gauge)

Instructions:

1. Disinfect the mushroom cap with alcohol to sterilize the surface.
2. Remove the stem from the mushroom cap and place it, gills or pores facing downwards, on a clean and sterile surface, such as a piece of aluminum foil or a petri dish.
3. Cover the mushroom cap with a clean container or lid and leave it for 12-24 hours in a clean and undisturbed area to allow the spores to drop onto the surface.
4. After the spores have fallen onto the surface, lift the lid and use a sterile scalpel or knife to scrape the spores from the surface and transfer them to a sterile container.
5. Add sterile water or saline solution to the container with the spores and mix the solution gently to disperse the spores evenly in the liquid. Aim for a concentration of 1 spore per 1 mL of solution.
6. Draw the spore solution into a sterile syringe using a sterile needle.
7. Remove the needle from the syringe and replace it with a clean, sterile needle for injection.
8. The spore syringe is now ready for use in inoculating a substrate for mushroom cultivation.

Note: It's important to maintain sterile conditions throughout the entire process to prevent contamination and ensure successful spore germination and growth. Additionally, it's recommended to use the spore syringe within a few weeks after preparation to ensure optimal viability and germination rates.

Here are the general steps to make liquid mushroom culture:

Materials:

- Mushroom strain or mycelium
- Sterilized liquid culture medium (e.g., potato dextrose broth, maltextract broth)
- Sterile Erlenmeyer flask or another sterile container with a lid
- Alcohol (70% isopropyl or ethanol)
- Flame source (e.g., alcohol burner, gas stove)

Instructions:

1. Sterilize the Erlenmeyer flask and liquid culture medium according to the appropriate protocol for your equipment and materials.
2. In a sterile environment such as a laminar flow hood or a still air box, flame sterilize the lid of the flask and the neck of the flask.
3. Using a sterile inoculation loop or syringe, transfer a small piece of mycelium or a small number of spores into the sterilized liquid culture medium.
4. Quickly seal the flask with the sterilized lid and shake the flask gently to distribute the inoculum throughout the medium.
5. Incubate the flask in a sterile and controlled environment, such as a growth chamber, at the appropriate temperature and humidity for the mushroom species or strain.
6. Monitor the culture for signs of growth, such as visible mycelium, and gently

shake the flask to distribute it throughout the medium or place it on a magnetic stirrer.

7. Use the liquid culture to inoculate substrates for mushroom cultivation or to create more liquid cultures through the process of sub-culturing.

Note: It's important to maintain sterile conditions throughout the entire process to prevent contamination and ensure successful growth of the mycelium. Additionally, it's recommended to use the liquid culture within afew weeks after preparation to ensure optimal viability and growth rates.

Here are recipes for two common liquid culture media used in mushroomcultivation:

1. Potato Dextrose Broth (PDB)

Ingredients:

- 200 g potatoes, peeled and chopped
- 20 g dextrose
- 1 L distilled water
- pH adjuster (e.g., 1 M HCl or NaOH)
- Autoclavable Erlenmeyer flask or another sterile container witha lid

Instructions:

1. Add the chopped potatoes and dextrose to a pot of distilled waterand bring to a boil. Simmer for 30 minutes, stirring occasionally. Filter the potato/dextrose mixture through a sterilized filter paper orcheesecloth to remove any solid particles.
2. Adjust the pH of the liquid to 5.6-5.8 using a pH adjuster.
3. Transfer the liquid to an autoclavable Erlenmeyer flask or othersterile

container with a lid.

4. Sterilize the liquid culture medium in an autoclave or pressure cookeraccording to the appropriate protocol for your equipment and materials.

5. Allow the medium to cool to room temperature before inoculatingwith mushroom mycelium or spores.

2. Malt Extract Broth (MEB)

Ingredients:

- 20 g malt extract
- 20 g dextrose
- 1 L distilled water
- pH adjuster (e.g., 1 M HCl or NaOH)
- Autoclavable Erlenmeyer flask or another sterile container witha lid

Instructions:

1. Add the malt extract and dextrose to a pot of distilled water and stiruntil dissolved.

2. Adjust the pH of the liquid to 5.6-5.8 using a pH adjuster.

3. Transfer the liquid to an autoclavable Erlenmeyer flask or other sterilecontainer with a lid. Sterilize the liquid culture medium in an autoclave or pressure cooker according to the appropriate protocol for your equipment and materials.

4. Allow the medium to cool to room temperature before inoculatingwith mushroom mycelium or spores.

Note: These recipes can be adjusted depending on the specific mushroomspecies or strain being cultivated. Additionally, it's important to maintain sterile conditions throughout the entire process to prevent contamination and ensure successful growth of the mycelium.

CHAPTER NINE:

Cultivating Mushrooms on Logs

Growing mushrooms on logs is a popular and sustainable method thatallows for outdoor cultivation. Here are the basic steps to grow mushrooms on logs:

1. Choose your logs: Select fresh hardwood logs from trees such as oak, maple, or beech. The logs should be between 3-8 inches (7.5-20 cm) in diameter and around 3-4 feet (0.9-1.2 m) in length.

2. Prepare the logs: Cut the logs to length and remove any branches or bark. Use an 8 mm drill to create holes in the logs, spaced 4-6 inches (10-15 cm) apart and 1-2 inches (2.5-5 cm) deep.

3. Inoculate the logs: Inoculate the logs by inserting mushroom spawn into the holes. The spawn can be purchased or made from spores. Seal the holes with wax to prevent contamination.

4. Incubate the logs: Store the inoculated logs in a cool, dark, and humid place, such as a shaded area in your backyard. Keep the logs moist by spraying them with water regularly and cover them with plastic sheeting or burlap to retain moisture.

5. Wait for colonization: After a few months, the mycelium will begin to colonize the logs. The logs should be fully colonized within 6-12 months, depending on the species of mushroom and the temperature.

6. Induce fruiting: Once the logs are fully colonized, move them to a sunny area and lean them against a fence or wall. Soak the logs in water for 24 hours to trigger fruiting. You can repeat this process every 2-4 weeks, depending on the weather conditions. Harvest the mushrooms: Mushrooms will begin to grow from the holes in the logs. Harvest them by gently twisting them off the log orcutting them with a sharp knife.

7. Repeat the process: After harvesting, let the logs rest for a few weeksbefore repeating the process with new spawns and fresh logs.

It's important to note that different types of mushrooms may have specificrequirements for temperature, humidity, and light, so it's important to research the specific needs of the mushroom species you are cultivating.

CHAPTER TEN:

Cultivating Mushrooms on Sawdust and Bran

Here are general steps to cultivate mushrooms on sawdust and bran:

Materials:

- Sawdust (hardwood or softwood)
- Bran (wheat or rice)
- Mushroom spawn or liquid culture
- Large pot or pressure cooker for sterilization
- Plastic bags or other containers for growing
- Perforated bag clamps or tape
- Water spray bottle
- Incubation chamber or space (e.g., closet, cupboard)

Instructions:

1. Mix the sawdust and bran together in a large container in the following ratio: 4 parts sawdust to 1 part bran.
2. Add enough water to the mixture to moisten it evenly without making it too wet or too dry. The ideal moisture level is when the mixture can be squeezed, and water droplets are released, but no excess water runs out.
3. Sterilize the sawdust and bran mixture in a large pot or pressure cooker for at least 2 hours at 15 PSI. Let it cool to room temperature before inoculating.
4. Inoculate the sawdust and bran mixture with mushroom spawn or liquid culture. Mix the spawn or culture thoroughly into the mixture until it's evenly distributed.
5. Transfer the inoculated mixture into plastic bags or other containers with perforated holes to allow for air exchange. Seal the bags or containers with perforated bag clamps or tape.
6. Incubate the bags or containers in a warm, dark, and humid environment, such as a closet or cupboard, for about 2-4 weeks until the mycelium has colonized the substrate.

7. After the mycelium has fully colonized the substrate, make small holes or slits in the bags or containers to allow the mushrooms to grow out. Spray the substrate with water daily to maintain humidity levels.

8. Harvest the mushrooms when they are fully grown and ready for consumption.

Note: Different mushroom species may require slightly different substrate preparation methods and environmental conditions for optimal growth. It'simportant to research and follow the specific requirements for the mushroom species you are cultivating.

To make sawdust bran spawn for mushrooms, you will need to followthese steps:

Supplementing sawdust bran spawn is important to provide the necessarynutrients for the mushrooms to grow. Here are some ways you can supplement your sawdust bran spawn:

1. Add additional nutrients: You can supplement your sawdust bran spawn by adding additional nutrients such as gypsum, calcium carbonate, or soybean meal. These supplements will provide additional nitrogen, calcium, and other nutrients that are essential formushroom growth.

2. Use grain spawn: Grain spawn can be mixed with sawdust bran spawn to provide additional nutrients and increase the colonization rate. Grain spawn is high in carbohydrates and protein, which are important for mushroom growth.

3. Add coffee grounds: Coffee grounds are a great source of nitrogen and can be added to the sawdust bran spawn to supplement its nutrient content. They should be used in moderation, however, as too much coffee can lower the pH level and make the substrate too acidic for mushroom growth.

4. Use other organic materials: Other organic materials such as straw, corn cobs, or horse manure can also be used to supplement sawdust bran spawn. These materials should be properly sterilized before use to prevent contamination.

5. Adjust the pH level: The pH level of the substrate is important for mushroom growth. If the pH is too high or too low, the mushrooms may not grow properly. You can adjust the pH level by adding lime to raise it or sulfur to lower it.

It's important to note that the specific supplementation methods may vary depending on the type of mushroom you are trying to grow. It's always a good idea to research the specific requirements for the type of mushroom you want to grow to ensure the best possible growth and yield.

CHAPTER ELEVEN:

Cultivating Mushrooms on Straw

Here are the basic steps to cultivate mushrooms on straw:

1. Select and prepare the straw: Choose a high-quality straw, such as wheat or barley straw and chop it into small pieces. Soak the straw in water for 24 hours, and then drain it and let it dry for a few hours. The straw should be at around 65-75% moisture content.

2. Pasteurize the straw: Pasteurize the straw by placing it in a large pot or container and adding enough water to cover it. Heat the straw to 160- 180°F (70-82°C) for 1- 2 hours, and then let it cool.

3. Inoculate the straw: Inoculate the straw with mushroom spawn, which can be purchased or made from spores. Mix the spawn with the straw by hand, making sure it is evenly distributed.

4. Fill the bags: Fill plastic bags with the inoculated straw, leaving some space at the top for the mushrooms to grow. Fold the top of the bag and poke several small holes to allow air to circulate.

5. Incubate the bags: Incubate the bags in a warm, dark place for several weeks. The temperature should be around 75-85°F (24-30°C). During this time, the mycelium will grow throughout the straw.

6. Induce fruiting: Once the mycelium has fully colonized the straw, induce fruiting by exposing the bags to light and lowering the temperature to around 60-70°F (15-21°C). Mist the bags with water regularly to keep the humidity high.

7. Harvest the mushrooms: Mushrooms will begin to appear after a few days. Harvest them by gently twisting them off the substrate.

Before using straw for mushroom cultivation, it needs to be prepared. To do this, you can fill a 45-gallon drum with water and calcium hydroxide or calcium oxide. Mix well and allow to ferment for nine to twelve days. Straw will need to be turned over once a week. Once the straw is ready to be used, you can pack it in eight-inch x 12-inch PP bags.

There are several ways to prepare bulk substrate for mushroom cultivation. The easiest is through cold fermentation, which involves immersing straw or wood chips in water for a week. Then, once the straw is submerged, the aerobic bacteria that live on the substrate die off, leaving only the anaerobic bacteria. After about a week, you can remove the substrate from the water and let it dry. If you have time, you can also pasteurize the substrate by boiling it for an hour in hot water. You can use 55-gallon metal drums to do this. Sterilization kills beneficial microorganisms. Pasteurization will not kill off beneficial bacteria that will be useful for inoculation.

The spawn will be able to colonize the straw after seven to fourteen days. Keep the bales cool. They may be too hot for the mycelium, so place them in a cool dark location. Using a 3% hydrogen peroxide will help kill spores and mycelium that may compete with the mushroom spawn.

CHAPTER TWELVE:

Cultivation of Oyster Mushrooms

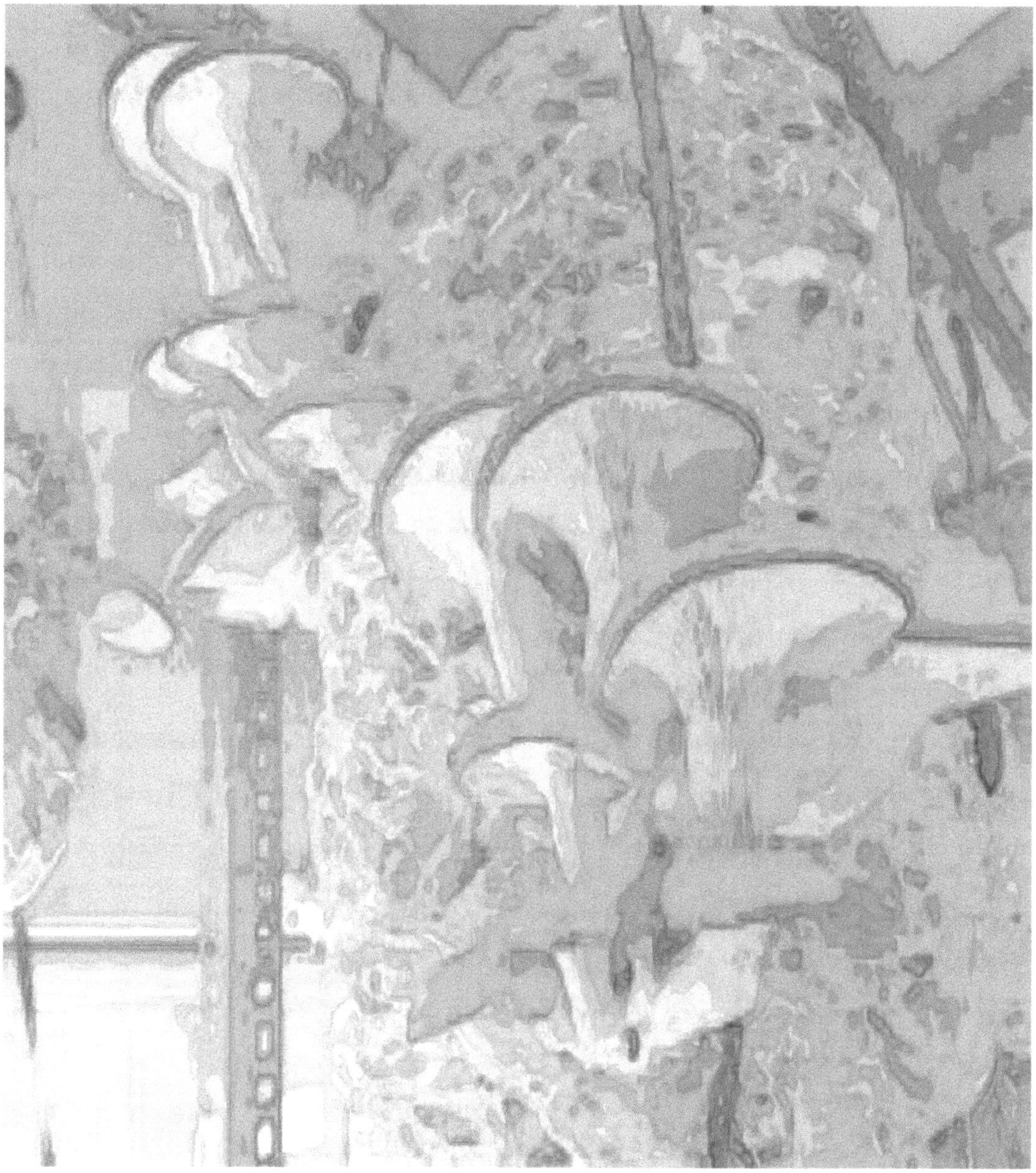

Oyster Mushroom Growth Parameters.

Oyster mushrooms (Pleurotus spp.) are one of the most popular and easiest mushrooms to grow. Here are the optimal growth parameters for oyster mushrooms:

1. Temperature: Oyster mushrooms grow best at a temperature range of 18-24°C (64-75°F) during the colonization phase and 12-18°C (5464°F) during the fruiting phase. If the temperature is too high, the mycelium growth will slow down or stop, while if it's too low, the mushrooms may not fruit.

2. Humidity: Oyster mushrooms require a high level of humidity during the fruiting phase, around 85-95%. Humidity can be maintained by frequent misting, watering, or using a humidifier. During the colonization phase, humidity is less critical, but it should not be too low to prevent drying out the substrate.

3. Light: Oyster mushrooms require light to induce fruiting, but they do not need direct sunlight. Indirect or diffused natural light or low-intensity artificial light sources are sufficient to stimulate fruiting.

4. Substrate: Oyster mushrooms can be grown on a variety of substrates, but the most used are straw, sawdust, and hardwood logs. The substrate should be free of contaminants, have a proper moisture level, and be properly sterilized or pasteurized before inoculation with mushroom spawn.

5. pH: Oyster mushrooms prefer a slightly acidic substrate with a pH range of 6.0-7.5.

6. CO_2 concentration: High levels of carbon dioxide (CO_2) inhibit the growth and development of oyster mushrooms, so proper ventilation is essential during fruiting. Adequate air exchange will also help prevent the accumulation of ethylene, which can negatively affect fruiting.

By controlling these parameters, you can optimize the growth and fruiting of oyster mushrooms and achieve a successful harvest.

How do I cultivate oyster mushrooms on straw?

Growing oyster mushrooms on straw is a simple and affordable method that requires minimal equipment. Here are the basic steps to grow oyster mushrooms on straw:

1. Prepare the straw: Use fresh, clean, and untreated straw. Cut the straw into pieces of around 4-6 inches (10-15 cm) in length. Soak thestraw in water for 12-24 hours to hydrate and soften it.

2. Pasteurize the straw: Pasteurization is the process of heating the straw to kill any competing bacteria and fungi that may interfere withmushroom growth. There are different methods of pasteurization, but a common one is to transfer the wet straw to a large pot or container and heat it to 60-70°C (140-160°F) for 1-2 hours.

3. Inoculate the straw: Once the straw has been pasteurized, allow it to cool down to room temperature. Inoculate the straw by mixing in oyster mushroom spawn, which can be purchased or obtained from aprevious batch of mushrooms. Use around 5-10% spawn by weight, depending on the quality of the spawn and the desired colonization speed.

4. Pack the straw: Pack the inoculated straw tightly into plastic bags orcontainers with small holes punched for ventilation. Leave some room at the top for the mushrooms to grow. Seal the bags or containers with a twist tie or tape.

5. Incubate the bags: Store the bags or containers in a dark, warm, and humid place, such as a closet or basement. Ideal temperature for incubation is around 18-24°C (64-75°F). Keep the bags or containers well-ventilated to prevent the accumulation of CO_2. Colonization shouldtake around 1-2 weeks.

6. Induce fruiting: Once the straw is fully colonized with white mycelium, it is time to induce fruiting. Cut or poke small holes in the bags or containers to allow for fruiting. Place the bags or containers in a well-lit area with indirect sunlight and a temperature range of 1218°C (54-64°F) and high humidity (around 85-95%).

7. Harvest the mushrooms: Mushrooms will start to appear after a few days or weeks. Harvest the mushrooms by gently twisting them off the substrate or cutting them with a sharp knife. Allow the substrate to rest for a few weeks before repeating the process with new spawn and fresh straw.

Growing oyster mushrooms on straw is a fun and rewarding activity that can yield a bountiful harvest of delicious and nutritious mushrooms. For more information, see chapter eleven.

Cultivation of Oyster Mushrooms on Sawdust and Ban

Cultivating oyster mushrooms on sawdust and bran is a relatively simple process that can be done at home or on a larger scale. Here are the basicsteps:

Materials needed:

- Oyster mushroom spawn
- Sawdust
- Bran
- Water
- Large pot or container with lid
- Plastic bags or containers for fruiting
- Sterilization equipment (pressure cooker or autoclave)
- Thermometer
- Spray bottle

Instructions:

1. Sterilize the sawdust and bran by boiling them in water or using a pressure cooker or autoclave. This is important to kill any bacteria orfungi that could compete with your oyster mushrooms.
2. Once the sawdust and bran are sterilized, mix them together in a large pot or container. The ratio should be roughly four parts sawdust to1 part bran.
3. Add enough water to the mixture so that it is damp but not drippingwet. Use a thermometer to make sure the temperature is around 7075°F (21-24°C).
4. Once the mixture has cooled to room temperature, add the oystermushroom spawn. Mix it in thoroughly.

5. Transfer the mixture to plastic bags or containers for fruiting. Pokesmall holes in the bags or containers to allow for air circulation.

6. Keep the bags or containers in a warm, dark place for 10-14 days.During this time, the mycelium will colonize the substrate.

7. After 10-14 days, move the bags or containers to a cooler, well-lit area. The mycelium will begin to form mushrooms. Spray the bags orcontainers with water regularly to keep the humidity high.

8. Harvest the mushrooms when they are fully grown. Cut them off atthe base and use them in your favorite recipes.

Note: Oyster mushrooms grow best at temperatures between 60-75°F (1524°C) and humidity levels between 80-90%. If you live in a dry climate,you may need to mist the bags or containers more often to keep the humidity high.

Cultivating Oyster Mushrooms on Logs

Growing oyster mushrooms on logs is a popular method of cultivation that requires a bit of patience but yields great results. Here are the basic steps to grow oyster mushrooms on logs:

1. Choose your logs: Oyster mushrooms can grow on a variety of hardwoods, such as oak, beech, poplar, or birch. The logs should befresh and untreated, free of cracks and mold, and cut into 3-4 feet(90-120 cm) in length and 3-6 inches (7-15 cm) in diameter.

2. Inoculate the logs: Once you have your logs, you need to inoculate them with oyster mushroom spawn. The spawn can be purchased or obtained from a previous batch of mushrooms. You can use a drill tomake 8 mm holes of around 1 inch (2.5 cm) in diameter and 3-4 inches (7-10 cm) apart on the log and insert the spawn into the holes.

3. Seal the holes: After the spawn has been inserted, seal the holes with wax or melted

paraffin. This will help prevent competing fungi and bacteria from colonizing the log.

4. Incubate the logs: Once the logs have been inoculated, they need tobe kept in a cool, dark, and humid place for about 6-12 months to allow the mycelium to colonize the log. You can stack the logs in a shady spot in your garden or in a container or raised bed that provides good drainage.

5. Induce fruiting: After the mycelium has colonized the log, it is time to induce fruiting. To do this, you need to shock the log by exposing it to colder temperatures and moisture. Soak the logs in cold water for 24-48 hours, then remove them from the water and place them in a shady spot with indirect sunlight and high humidity (around 8595%). The ideal temperature range for fruiting is around 12-18°C (54-64°F).

6. Harvest the mushrooms: Mushrooms will start to appear after a few days or weeks. Harvest the mushrooms by gently twisting them off the log or cutting them with a sharp knife. Allow the log to rest for afew weeks before repeating the process with new spawns and fresh logs.

Growing oyster mushrooms on logs is a fun and sustainable way to cultivate this delicious and nutritious fungus. With a bit of patience andcare, you can enjoy a bountiful harvest of oyster mushrooms from youown backyard.

Health Benefits of Oyster Mushrooms.

Oyster mushrooms are not only delicious, but they also offer several healthbenefits. Here are some of the potential health benefits of oyster mushrooms:

1. Nutrient-rich: Oyster mushrooms are low in calories but high in nutrients, including protein, fiber, vitamins B and D, and mineralssuch as iron, potassium, and selenium.

2. Anti-inflammatory properties: Oyster mushrooms contain compounds such as ergothioneine and polysaccharides that have been shown to have anti-inflammatory effects. This makes them potentiallybeneficial in reducing inflammation-related health issues such as arthritis, heart disease, and diabetes.

3. Immune system support: Some compounds found in oystermushrooms, such as beta-glucans, may have immune-boosting properties that can help enhance the body's ability to fightinfections and diseases.

4. Antioxidant properties: Oyster mushrooms contain high levels of antioxidants such as polyphenols, which can help protect cells fromdamage caused by harmful free radicals and oxidative stress.

5. Cholesterol-lowering effects: Studies have suggested that consumingoyster mushrooms may help lower cholesterol levels, which is beneficial for heart health.

6. Anti-cancer properties: Some research has suggested that oyster mushrooms may have anti-cancer properties due to their high levelsof antioxidants and other compounds that can help inhibit tumor growth and induce cancer cell death.

7. Overall, oyster mushrooms offer a range of potential health benefits andcan be a nutritious and tasty addition to your diet.

Labeling Logs with Mushroom Type and Date Inoculated

One way to ensure the freshness of your mushrooms is to label the logs with the type of mushroom you grew, the date of inoculation, and the location. These three things are important to properly label your mushrooms because they will begin to decompose over time. A good place to store logs is under a tree or bush, as they will lose their original weight. The north side of your homestead is a good choice. If you have anabundance of fungi, consider drying them.

The best time to inoculate your logs is during the fall or winter when the trees are dormant. Select logs that are four to ten inches in diameter andtwo to five feet long. If you cannot find a log with a diameter this big, you can also inoculate hardwood tree stumps. If you have a tree stump that is afew feet tall, you can use it as your inoculated logs.

If you are growing oyster mushrooms, you should inoculate enough logs toensure that your harvest will be a regular cycle. You can then stagger harvests, so you can harvest a quarter of your logs one week and ten percent the next. This way, you will be guaranteed mushrooms all season long. A three-foot log should produce between two to three pounds of mushrooms every fruiting cycle. For best results, soak logs in a natural water source, as chlorinated municipal water will kill the mycelium.

Chapter Thirteen:

Cultivating Shiitake Mushrooms

Growth Parameters of Shitakes

Shiitake mushrooms are a popular type of edible fungus that can be cultivated indoors or outdoors. Here are some of the growth parameters that are important for shiitake mushroom cultivation:

1. Substrate: Shiitake mushrooms can grow on a variety of substrates, including sawdust, hardwood logs, and wood chips. Sawdust and wood chips are often used for indoor cultivation, while logs are used for outdoor cultivation.

2. Temperature: The ideal temperature range for shiitake mushroom growth is between 20-28°C (68-82°F). However, different strains may have different temperature requirements, so it's important to choose a strain that is well-suited to your growing conditions.

3. Humidity: Shiitake mushrooms require high humidity levels to grow, with an ideal range of around 80-90%. This can be achieved by regularly misting the substrate or using a humidifier.

4. Light: Shiitake mushrooms do not require light to grow, but they should be kept in a well-lit area to help prevent contamination.

5. Air circulation: Good air circulation is important for shiitake mushroom growth to prevent the buildup of carbon dioxide and to promote the exchange of oxygen and other gases. This can be achieved by using fans or ventilation systems.

6. Spawn rate: The spawn rate for shiitake mushrooms can vary depending on the substrate and growing conditions. A spawn rate of 5-10% is generally recommended

for sawdust or wood chips, while a higher spawn rate of 15-20% may be needed for logs.

7. Harvesting: Shiitake mushrooms can be harvested when the caps are fully expanded, usually within 7-14 days of fruiting. To harvest, gently twist the mushroom stem and pull it away from the substrate.

By carefully controlling these growth parameters, you can successfully cultivate shiitake mushrooms and enjoy their delicious flavor and health benefits.

How to Cultivate Shiitake Mushrooms on Logs

To grow shiitake mushrooms on logs, you'll need to follow some basic guidelines. Read on to learn about the benefits of growing shiitake mushrooms on logs, choosing a healthy tree, watering shiitake logs, and harvesting shiitake mushrooms. You'll have plenty of fun while doing this!

1. Cut 3"-6" hardwood trees between December and March to 3'-4' length. Remove all branches and make sure the bark is intact without being damaged and free of fungus and contamination.

2. With an 8mm drill bit or 5/16inch drill bit, drill 1" deep holes 6" apart and 2" between holes in each row

3. Fill holes with either dowels or sawdust. When using dowels, you may either use spiral grooved (pictured) or straight grooved, and metric size 8mmx25mm or standard 5/16inch x 1inch. Both types of dowels work well for growing mushroom plug spawn and can be used either with either an 8mm drill bit or a 5/16 inch drill bit. Each dowel is hammered in until it is flush with the surface of the log. If you are using sawdust spawn, you will need to use an inoculation tool. Make sure that the hole is completely full of sawdust.

4. Finally, cover each inoculated hole with wax to protect the spawn from drying out, being eaten by insects, and keeping contamination spores from entering the logs.

5. Stack the logs in a shaded environment under conifer trees is ideal, or you can use 40-60% shade cloth if you do not have a tree canopy.

Here are a few things you should know before you begin growing shiitake mushrooms on logs. First, you must know when to harvest the logs. They should be clean and have intact bark. You can cut your own logs or contact an arborist or tree service to get them for you. They will sell you their logs rather than chip them. In addition, you can buy logs from a commercial shiitake grower if you have access to their supply.

Growing shiitake mushrooms on logs can produce fruit 3 to four times per year. The first year's harvest is usually lower than the other years, but the yield increases each year after the shiitake mycelium has established itself within the log. You should soak the log overnight in ice water. You should water the logs 2-3 times per week. Make sure to use ice water when the temperature drops below freezing.

The first step in growing shiitake mushrooms is to choose healthy trees. A good tree contains a high moisture content, which is vital for the fungus to grow. Furthermore, a healthy tree will produce a more flavorful mushroom that lasts for longer.

In addition to the flavor and nutritional benefits of shiitake mushrooms, traditional cultivation also provides a good source of income on your forest land. The market price for a pound of shiitake mushrooms can reach as high as $16 if you sell it direct to consumers. It can be even more profitable if you choose to sell it wholesale. The first step in growing shiitake mushrooms is to start with a freshly felled log that is at least three inches in diameter. It should not have been sitting around for more than two weeks, as this will allow the mycelium to colonize the log. The log should be moist and exposed to airflow, as this will encourage fungus growth. Shiitake mushrooms are not competitive outside of their native habitat, so a moist log is ideal.

Watering shiitake logs when cultivating mushrooms should occur every week to a day. Shiitake mushrooms grow best in moist areas, so they require lots of moisture. You can harvest up to 5 flushes of mushrooms in a single season! Depending on the variety, you can choose to harvest shiitake mushrooms at any time of the year. If you don't plan to harvest them regularly, harvesting them at the end of the season is a viable option.

If you are growing in an outdoor climate, you can place the logs inside plastic bags to protect them from the elements. Before you place them in the log, be sure to disinfect the surrounding areas and your hands. Shiitake mushrooms do not grow well in warm or humid conditions and must be protected from the sun. This means that they should be protected from excessive heat. Breathable fabric should be placed over the logs, as plastic tarps can attract mold.

They will not grow on live trees or deadfall, as the spawn does not like these. Also, do not harvest mushrooms on trees with lichens.

Freshly felled or just-trimmed trees are best. You can determine whether a log is large enough to contain a large quantity of sapwood by inspecting the end of the log. In most cases, the ratio of heartwood to sapwood will be the same as that of trees in a specific area. If there is only a small amount of heartwood, the log will likely not produce mushrooms for more than two years.

Log-grown shiitake mushrooms have several benefits. They require less capital and can produce additional income for the farmer. These mushrooms are also considered superior to their sawdust-grown counterparts in terms of taste, nutritional value, and medicinal value.

Cultivating Shiitake Mushrooms on Sawdust and Bran

Growing shiitake mushrooms on sawdust and bran is a common method used by commercial growers and hobbyists alike. Here are the general steps you can follow:

1. Obtain shiitake mushroom spawn: You can purchase shiitake mushroom spawn from a reputable supplier. It's best to use a spawn that's been specifically designed for growing shiitake mushrooms on sawdust and bran.

2. Prepare the substrate: Mix the sawdust and bran together in a large container or bag. The ideal ratio is typically five parts sawdust to 1 part bran. Add enough water to moisten the mixture thoroughly but avoid making it too wet. You want the mixture to be about as moist as a wrung-out sponge.

3. Sterilize the substrate: Place the sawdust and bran mixture into bags and sterilize it by heating it in a pressure cooker or autoclave. This will kill off any bacteria or other microorganisms that could compete with the shiitake mycelium.

4. Inoculate the substrate: Once the bags have cooled, inject them with the shiitake mushroom spawn using a sterile syringe. Make sure the spawn is evenly distributed throughout the substrate.

5. Incubate the bags: Keep the bags in a warm, dark, and humid place (between 65- and 80 degrees Fahrenheit) for about 4-6 weeks. During this time, the mycelium will grow throughout the substrate, colonizing it.

6. Stimulate fruiting: Once the mycelium has fully colonized the substrate, you'll need to stimulate fruiting by exposing the bags to cooler temperatures (between 50 and 60 degrees Fahrenheit) and higher humidity (around 90%). You can do this by placing the bags in a humid environment (like a greenhouse) and misting them regularly.

7. Harvest the mushrooms: After a few weeks of exposure to cooler temperatures and higher humidity, small, pinhead-sized mushrooms will start to appear. These will

grow and mature over the course of a few days, and you can harvest them when the caps are fully opened and the gills are exposed.

Store the sawdust blocks in a humid environment and mist them with distilled water or bottled water once a day. In addition, fresh air is necessary to maintain the spores.

There are several methods for inoculating shiitake spores on sawdust blocks. The best materials are hardwood sawdust, oat bran, and wheat bran. The spores need 10-14 days to colonize a sawdust block. They grow well in a range of temperatures but are most successful when they are grown at high humidity.

After mixing the inoculant with sawdust, seal the block with a rubber band or tie.

Shiitake mushrooms are fungal spores. Because they are not competitive with other fungi, you should pick a healthy log that has a lot of sapwood. You can easily determine whether your tree has enough sapwood by looking at the end of its log. In general, trees in your area have a similar ratio of sapwood to heartwood. If the sapwood is light, the log will produce mushrooms in less than two years.

When growing shiitake mushrooms in bags, you should start by creating a fruiting chamber, which is connected to a fan and humidifier that run on a timer. Every hour or so, fresh air is allowed to come in, which will stimulate fruiting. The humidity and temperature should remain between 20 and 30 deg C during this stage. However, the block should not be exposed to too much light, as this will cause the mushrooms to become wet.

After two or three months, you should see signs of growth in the spawn block. It will start off as a thin white mycelium. Some will even look like white hairs. The growing mycelium will begin to brown, and you can harvest them before the spores drop. As the mycelium ages and becomes brown, shiitake mushrooms will start fruiting. As the spawn starts to turn brown, you should remove the sawdust blocks and place them in a cool, dark place.

Health and Medicinal Benefits of Shitake Mushrooms

Shiitake mushrooms are not only delicious but also have many potential health benefits. Here are some of the health benefits associated with consuming shiitake mushrooms:

1. Boost immune function: Shiitake mushrooms contain compounds called beta-glucans, which have been shown to stimulate the immune system and improve its ability to fight infections.

2. Lower cholesterol levels: Shiitake mushrooms contain eritadenine, a compound that has been shown to lower cholesterol levels in animal studies.

3. Support cardiovascular health: Shiitake mushrooms contain compounds that may help reduce inflammation, which is a risk factor for heart disease. They may also help lower blood pressure.

4. Aid in weight management: Shiitake mushrooms are low in calories and fat but high in fiber, which can help you feel full and satisfied after eating, making them a good addition to a weight management plan.

5. Support brain function: Shiitake mushrooms contain compounds that may help protect the brain from damage and reduce the risk of cognitive decline.

6. Have anti-cancer properties: Some studies have suggested that shiitake mushrooms may have anti-cancer properties due to their ability to stimulate the immune system and inhibit the growth of cancer cells.

It is worth noting that while shiitake mushrooms have many potential health benefits, more research is needed to fully understand the extent of these benefits and how they may vary among individuals. Nonetheless, incorporating shiitake mushrooms into your diet is a great way to add flavor and potential health benefits to your meals.

CHAPTER FOURTEEN:

How to Cultivate Cordyceps Militarus

Growth Parameters of Cordyceps Militarus

Cordyceps militarus is a species of mushroom that is highly valued for its medicinal and nutritional properties. It is a saprophytic fungus that is commonly found growing on insects but can also be cultivated on a variety of substrates. Here are some of the growth parameters of Cordyceps militarus:

1. Temperature: Cordyceps militarus grows best at a temperature range of 20-30°C (68-86°F). However, it can tolerate temperatures as low as 10°C (50°F) and as high as 35°C (95°F).

2. Light: Cordyceps militarus is a phototropic fungus, meaning that it responds to light. It grows best in a well-lit area, but direct sunlight should be avoided as it can be harmful to the mycelium.

3. pH: Cordyceps militarus prefers a slightly acidic pH range of 5.5-6.5, but it can also grow in a pH range of 5-7.

4. Substrate: Cordyceps militarus can be grown on a variety of substrates, including grains, sawdust, and agricultural waste products. Rice, barley, and soybean are some of the most used substrates.

5. Humidity: Cordyceps militarus requires high humidity levels to grow, with optimal humidity levels between 70-80%. However, it is important to ensure that there is adequate air circulation to prevent the growth of mold and other contaminants.

6. CO2: Cordyceps militarus prefers a low concentration of carbon dioxide in the

growing environment. CO2 levels should be kept below 0.3% to ensure optimal growth.

7. Nutrients: Cordyceps militarus requires a source of nitrogen, carbon, and other essential nutrients to grow. Nutrient-rich substrates such as soybean, wheat bran, and cornmeal are often used to provide these nutrients.

8. Overall, cultivating Cordyceps militarus requires careful attention to the growth parameters mentioned above to ensure optimal growth and yield.

Cultivating Cordyceps Militarus

Cordyceps militarus is a species of cordyceps mushroom that is easier to cultivate than other species, such as Cordyceps sinensis. Here are the general steps for cultivating Cordyceps militarus:

1. Obtain a pure culture: The first step in cultivating Cordyceps militaris is to obtain a pure culture of the fungus. You can purchase a culture from a mushroom supplier or obtain one from the wild.

2. Prepare a substrate: Cordyceps militarus can grow on a variety of substrates, such as rice, wheat, or barley. Sterilize the substrate by boiling it for 30-60 minutes, then let it cool to room temperature.

3. Inoculate the substrate: Once the substrate is cooled, inoculate it with the pure culture of Cordyceps militarus. Spread the culture evenly over the surface of the substrate, then cover it with a layer of vermiculite to help maintain moisture.

4. Incubate the substrate: Place the inoculated substrate in a warm, humid place

(around 77-86 degrees Fahrenheit and 75-85% humidity) to allow the mycelium to grow. This can take anywhere from a few days to several weeks, depending on the conditions.

5. Transfer to a fruiting container: Once the mycelium has colonized the substrate, transfer it to a fruiting container. This could be a plastic bag or a tray with a lid. Make sure the container is ventilated and has holes for air exchange.

6. Initiate fruiting: To initiate fruiting, lower the temperature to around 68-72 degrees Fahrenheit and increase humidity to around 85-95%. You can also expose the substrate to light to encourage fruiting.

7. Harvest the mushrooms: Cordyceps militarus mushrooms can take several weeks to grow and mature. When they're ready to harvest, carefully cut them off the substrate using a sterilized knife or scissors

Overall, cultivating Cordyceps militarus is a relatively straightforward process compared to other species of cordyceps mushrooms. However, it
still requires careful attention to temperature, humidity, and other environmental factors to ensure successful growth.

Cultivating Cordyceps Militarus

Growing Cordyceps militarus is an environmentally friendly option that will not involve any insecticides or fertilizers. It also allows you to become vegan, as there is no need to harvest the fungus from insects. Plus, you can use the same medicinal benefits as C. sinensis without paying the high price and wasting a limited resource. Additionally, growing Cordyceps militarus in jars will allow you to reap the health benefits of the fungus in mass amounts.

Using a waste drink bottle as cultivated container of Cordyceps militarus is a practical way to grow the medicinal mushroom. Besides being environmentally friendly, this method improves product quality and saves costs. In addition, it contributes to the development of the low-carbon economy. Let us discuss more.

To successfully conduct aseptic cultivation of cordyceps militarus, sterile equipment is necessary. The sterilization process includes steam or dry heat. The multisensor module was sterilized by steam heat, and the lid of the jar incubator was covered with a HEPA membrane to minimize contamination.

Cordycep Substrate Recipes:

(Method 1):

Growing Cordyceps on Brown Rice or Grains

- 3 Whole eggs (including shells) blended well with a blender
- 1 Tbs Malt extract
- 1 Tbs Yeast extract

Instructions:

1. Fill with water until you reach 500ml, then blend again in blender.

2. Measure out thirty-five grams rice for each jar.

3. Wait until the foam is gone in solution.

4. Add 60-70 ml solution to each jar.

5. Add lids (with injection ports and filter) along with tinfoil and pressure cook at 15 psi for 60 minutes. Once cooled, inoculate each jar with 10-20 ccs of liquid culture.

6. Set the jars in a completely dark place, like in a box, at temperatures between 60-70F. (never above 70F).

7. After about 7-10 days, take them out of the dark and place in indirect sunlight (or artificial light) for about 12 hours per day to initiate fruiting while maintaining a temperature between 60-70F. (never above 70F). Over the next 4-5 weeks, the jars will change color to orange and start producing mushroom fruit bodies.

(Method 2)

Growing Cordyceps on Brown Rice (Can also use Grains) In a Qt size canning jar (or measuring cup), add:

- 100ml potato broth (boil a potato and strain out the water) or 5 grams of Potato / Corn starch (can also use Instant Potato Flakes)
- 15 grams Dextrose (or 2 tablespoons of Karo (corn) syrup)
- 5 grams of Yeast Extract (or Nutritional Yeast)
- 1 teaspoon of Gypsum (or Azomite)
- 3 grams Soya Peptone (or add 3 more grams of Yeast Extract or Nutritional Yeast)

Instructions:

1. Take your canning jar with all the ingredients added and finish filling it with water (I use hot tap water) to the 500ml mark.

2. Add a lid and shake it up to mix it very well. Get 6 Qt jars and add fifty grams of

brown rice to each one.

3. Split the liquid solution evenly into 6 Qt jars (83ml each) (If needed, weigh it out and divide by 6). This should total 100 ml per jar.

4. Add lids (with injection ports and filter) along with tinfoil and pressure cook at 15 psi for 60 minutes.

5. Once cooled, inoculate each jar with 10-20 cc's of liquid culture.

6. Set the jars in a completely dark place, like in a box, at temperatures between 60-70F. (never above 70F).

7. After about 7-10 days, take them out of the dark and place in indirect sunlight (or artificial light) for about 12 hours per day to initiate fruiting while maintaining a temperature between 60-70F. (never above 70F). Over the next 4-5 weeks, the jars will change color to orange and start producing mushroom fruit bodies.

Health Benefits of Cordyceps Militarus

Cordyceps is a type of fungus that has been used in traditional Chinese medicine for centuries. It is believed to have various health benefits, including:

1. Boosting the immune system: Cordyceps contains polysaccharides, which are believed to stimulate the immune system, helping the body fight off infections and diseases.

2. Increasing energy and reducing fatigue: Cordyceps is believed to improve oxygen utilization in the body, which can increase energy levels and reduce fatigue.

3. Improving respiratory function: Cordyceps is believed to improve lung function and oxygen uptake, making it helpful for people with respiratory conditions such as asthma and chronic obstructive pulmonary disease (COPD).

4. Lowering cholesterol: Some studies suggest that cordyceps may help lower LDL (bad) cholesterol levels and triglycerides, which can reduce the risk of heart disease.

5. Enhancing athletic performance: Cordyceps is believed to improve endurance and reduce fatigue, making it popular among athletes.

6. Anti-inflammatory effects: Some studies have suggested that cordyceps has anti-inflammatory effects, which may be helpful for people with inflammatory conditions such as arthritis.

It is important to note that while there is some evidence to support these health benefits, more research is needed to fully understand the effects of cordyceps. As with any supplement, it is also important to speak with a healthcare professional before taking cordyceps, especially if you are taking other medications or have underlying health conditions.

CHAPTER FIFTEEN:

Maitake Mushroom Cultivation

Growth Parameters of Maitakes

Maitake mushrooms (Grifola frondosa) are a popular edible and medicinal mushroom that can be grown in a variety of cultivation environments. Here are some of the key growth parameters for maitake mushrooms:

1. Temperature: Maitake mushrooms grow best in cool temperatures between 55-65 degrees Fahrenheit (12-18 degrees Celsius), with 60 degrees Fahrenheit (15 degrees Celsius) being optimal.

2. Humidity: Maitake mushrooms require high humidity levels to grow. Ideal humidity ranges from 80-90%, with 85% being optimal.

3. Light: Maitake mushrooms do not require light to grow, but exposing them to a light source can help induce fruiting.

4. Substrate: Maitake mushrooms can be grown on a variety of substrates, including sawdust, hardwood logs, and straw. They prefer substrates that are high in lignin and cellulose.

5. Spawn type: Maitake mushrooms can be grown using grain spawn or sawdust spawn. Sawdust spawn is preferred by many growers because it is easier to work with.

6. Fruiting: Maitake mushrooms typically fruit in the fall but can be induced to fruit at other times of the year with the proper environmental conditions.

7. Harvesting: Maitake mushrooms can be harvested when the caps are fully developed and the edges begin to curl upwards. It's important to harvest the mushrooms before the caps flatten out, as this can indicate over-ripeness.

Overall, maitake mushrooms are relatively easy to grow and can be cultivated in a variety of environments. However, they do require careful attention to temperature, humidity, and substrate quality to ensure successful growth and fruiting.

Harvesting them is easy if you follow the growing instructions. The mushrooms will last for at least two weeks in a paper bag. You can also freeze your harvest for future use.

Cultivating Maitake Mushrooms on Logs

Growing maitake mushrooms on logs is a popular and traditional method of cultivation. Here are the general steps for cultivating maitake mushrooms on logs:

1. Obtain logs: Maitake mushrooms are typically grown on hardwood logs, such as oak or maple. The logs should be freshly cut, with a diameter of around 4-8 inches (10-20 cm) and a length of around 3-4 feet (0.9-1.2 meters).

2. Inoculate the logs: Inoculate the logs with maitake mushroom spawn by drilling holes in the logs and inserting the spawn plugs. The holes should be around 1 inch (2.5 cm) deep and spaced 4-6 inches (10-15 cm) apart.

3. Seal the holes: Once the spawn plugs are inserted, seal the holes with wax to prevent contamination.

4. Store the logs: Place the inoculated logs in a cool, shady area with high humidity. The logs should be kept off the ground to prevent contamination and decay.

5. Wait for colonization: The mycelium will take several months to fully colonize the logs, depending on environmental conditions.

6. Induce fruiting: Once the mycelium has colonized the logs, soak them in cold water for 24-48 hours to simulate rainfall and induce fruiting. You can also cut small notches in the bark to encourage fruiting.

7. Harvest the mushrooms: Maitake mushrooms will typically grow from the notches or cracks in the bark. Harvest the mushrooms when they are fully developed and the edges begin to curl upwards.

8. Repeat the process: After harvesting, allow the logs to rest for a few months before attempting to fruit them again. You can repeat the process of soaking and notching the logs to encourage further fruiting.

Overall, growing maitake mushrooms on logs is a rewarding and sustainable method of cultivation. However, it does require patience and careful attention to environmental conditions to ensure successful growth and fruiting.

When to harvest the coveted Maitake mushroom, late summer to early fall is the time to do so. Typically, they grow in the undergrowth of oak, maple, and elm trees. However, if you can't find any in your area, you can easily grow them yourself at home with a log or two. However, growing them outdoors requires more work and time than growing them indoors.

Another way to grow Maitake is by using a growing kit. These kits are convenient for kids to use and are easy to set up. The mushroom spawn will react like a spring when you remove it. You can also use the used kits to start your outdoor maitake mushroom cultivation. And if you're a complete novice, you can always buy a used kit and use it as a spawn. But for the most part, grow maitake mushrooms in bags! You'll be glad you did! You'll have a tasty harvest in no time! And when you finally get to enjoy the mushrooms that you grow, they'll be worth it.

To properly care for your maitake mushrooms, it's necessary to clean them after growing them in bags. As with any mushroom, these edibles are prone to dirt and other organic matter. This makes cleaning maitake mushrooms more difficult than other types. Pick off larger pieces of organic matter and soil using a soft brush. Once you've finished cleaning the mushrooms, rinse them well to remove any remaining dirt. You can also leave them for a few days before you plan to cook them.

Before harvesting the mushrooms, check for their freshness. The mushroom should be light gray to brown in color with plump fronds. Avoid the mushroom caps with a slimy film or moldy signs. Rinse them carefully with cold water. After the mushrooms are thoroughly soaked, pat them dry using paper towels. Do not chop or tear them; instead, carefully tear apart their caps. These mushrooms will retain their freshness much better than other mushrooms.

How to Cultivate Maitake Mushrooms on Sawdust and Bran

Growing maitake mushrooms on sawdust and bran is a popular and efficient method of cultivation. Here are the general steps for cultivating maitake mushrooms on sawdust and bran:

1. Prepare the substrate: Mix sawdust and bran in a ratio of 4:1 (sawdust: bran) in a large container. The sawdust should be hardwood sawdust, such as oak or maple.

2. Sterilize the substrate: Sterilize the substrate by steaming or pressure cooking it at 15 PSI for 90 minutes. This will kill any unwanted microorganisms that may be present.

3. Inoculate the substrate: Once the substrate has cooled, mix in the maitake mushroom spawn. The spawn should be evenly distributed throughout the substrate.

4. Incubate the substrate: Place the inoculated substrate in a plastic bag or container and incubate it at 70-75°F (21-24°C) in the dark for 2-4 weeks or until the mycelium has fully colonized the substrate.

5. Prepare the fruiting container: Once the substrate is fully colonized, transfer it to a fruiting container. The container can be a plastic bag or a plastic or metal container with small holes for ventilation.

6. Induce fruiting: Place the fruiting container in a cool, humid environment with a temperature between 55-65°F (12-18°C) and high humidity levels between 85-95%. You can also expose the container to a light source to help induce fruiting.

7. Harvest the mushrooms: Maitake mushrooms will typically grow from the substrate within 1-2 weeks after fruiting conditions are established. Harvest the mushrooms when they are fully developed and the edges begin to curl upwards.

8. Repeat the process: After harvesting, allow the substrate to rest for a few weeks before attempting to fruit it again. You can repeat the process of incubating and fruiting the substrate to encourage further mushroom growth.

Overall, growing maitake mushrooms on sawdust and bran is a relatively easy and efficient method of cultivation. However, it does require careful attention to environmental conditions to ensure successful growth and fruiting.

Maitake mushrooms also require indirect sunlight, but you will not need to provide it until the mushroom bodies start forming. To maintain humidity levels, mist spray irrigation is used. The mature mushrooms should be picked when their caps are about two inches in diameter. A sharp knife is essential for harvesting.

Maitake mushrooms are polypore fungi and are commonly found in oak or other woody areas in autumn. They can grow anywhere from a few inches to 36 inches in diameter. Their wavy pattern and brownish color can help you identify them. They grow best on wood and are especially common in oak savannahs. To grow them, they need an area with a moist environment with a lot of hardwood and some hardwood sawdust.

Health Benefits of Maitake Mushrooms

Maitake mushrooms (Grifola frondosa) are a type of edible mushroom that has been used for medicinal purposes in traditional Chinese and Japanese medicine for centuries. Here are some of the potential health benefits of maitake mushrooms:

1. Boosts immune function: Maitake mushrooms contain beta-glucans, which are polysaccharides that have been shown to stimulate the immune system. They may help improve the body's response to infections and diseases, as well as enhance the efficacy of vaccines.

2. Helps regulate blood sugar: Maitake mushrooms contain compounds that have been shown to improve insulin sensitivity and help regulate blood sugar levels. They may be beneficial for people with diabetes or other blood sugar disorders.

3. May have anticancer properties: Some studies suggest that maitake mushrooms may have anticancer properties, as they contain compounds that have been shown to inhibit the growth of cancer cells and stimulate the immune system's response to cancer. However, more research is needed to confirm these findings.

4. Improves cardiovascular health: Maitake mushrooms may help improve cardiovascular health by reducing cholesterol and triglyceride levels and improving blood flow. They may also help reduce inflammation, which is a risk factor for heart disease.

5. May improve cognitive function: Some studies suggest that maitake mushrooms may have neuroprotective properties and may help improve cognitive function. They may be beneficial for people with age-related cognitive decline or neurodegenerative disorders such as Alzheimer's disease.

6. Overall, maitake mushrooms are a nutritious and potentially beneficial addition to a healthy diet. However, it's important to note that more research is needed to fully understand their health benefits and potential side effects. As with any supplement or dietary change, it's best to talk to a healthcare provider before incorporating maitake mushrooms into your diet.

CHAPTER SIXTEEN:

Cultivating Reishi Mushrooms

Reishi Mushroom Growth Parameters

Reishi mushrooms (Ganoderma lucidum) are known for their medicinal properties and are used in traditional Chinese medicine. They can be grown on a variety of substrates, including logs, sawdust, and straw. Here are some key parameters to consider when growing reishi mushrooms:

1. Substrate: Reishi mushrooms can be grown on logs, sawdust, and straw. Sawdust and straw are the most common substrates used for indoor cultivation.

2. Spawn: Spawn is the mycelium of the reishi mushroom that is used to inoculate the substrate. It is typically grown on a grain-based medium, such as rye, wheat, or millet.

3. Temperature: Reishi mushrooms grow best at temperatures between 20°C and 27°C (68°F to 81°F). They can tolerate temperatures as low as 10°C (50°F) and as high as 35°C (95°F), but growth may be slower or less productive outside the optimal temperature range.

4. Humidity: Reishi mushrooms require high humidity levels to grow. Humidity levels should be maintained between 80% and 90%.

5. Light: Reishi mushrooms do not require light to grow, but they will fruit better if exposed to a small amount of light. Some growers use low-intensity fluorescent lighting to promote fruiting.

6. Air exchange: Good air exchange is important for healthy reishi mushroom growth. A fan or ventilation system can be used to maintain fresh air exchange.

7. pH: The pH of the substrate should be between 5.5 and 6.5 for optimal reishi mushroom growth.

8. Harvest: Reishi mushrooms can take several months to mature. They are typically harvested when the caps are fully developed and the edges start to turn upward.

Overall, growing reishi mushrooms can be a rewarding and beneficial hobby, but it requires attention to detail and consistent environmental conditions.

Cultivating Reishi Mushrooms on Logs

1. Cut 3"-6" hardwood trees between December and March to 3'-4' length. Remove all branches and make sure the bark is intact without being damaged and free of fungus and contamination.

2. , with an 8mm drill bit or 5/16inch drill bit, drill 1" deep holes 6" apart and 2" between holes in each row

3. Fill holes with either dowels or sawdust. When using dowels, you may either use spiral grooved (pictured) or straight grooved, and metric size 8mmx25mm or standard 5/16inch x 1inch. Both types of dowels work well for growing mushroom plug spawn and can be used either with either an 8mm drill bit or a 5/16 inch drill bit. Each dowel is hammered in until it is flush with the surface of the log. If you are using sawdust spawn, you will need to use an inoculation tool. Make sure that the hole is completely full of sawdust.

4. Finally, cover each inoculated hole with wax to protect the spawn from drying out, being eaten by insects, and keeping contamination spores from entering the logs.

5. Stack the logs in a shaded environment under conifer trees is ideal, or you can use 40-60% shade cloth if you do not have a tree canopy.

Reishi mushrooms grow best in moist and warm conditions. The spawn form at the top of the substrate. To plant Reishi mushrooms, cover a block with bran and sawdust, mix well, and place in the sun. A year after inoculation, the log should start fruiting. If you'd like to harvest Reishi mushrooms in the spring, wait until it's in the full fruiting stage. Harvesting Reishi at this stage will be much easier, though.

If you're growing Reishi outdoors, be sure to choose well-drained sandy soil and a layer of gravel to deter insects from attacking mushroom spawn. Reishi prefers a moist, warm environment. Once you've established a moist growing medium, you can plant Reishi on a log or in a bag of sawdust substrate. This method is faster and more enjoyable than cultivating on logs.

There are a few things to keep in mind when preparing a substrate for Reishi mushroom cultivation. One of the most important factors is the ratio of the bran and sawdust. In some cases, different types of bran are better than others. For example, rice bran was less productive than sawdust, and the ratio of sawdust to bran was lower than wheat bran. A variety of substrates may increase your mushroom yield.

Reishi mushroom fruiting occurs in the summer after inoculation. They start off as antlers and flatten into conks. You can harvest Reishi at any stage, but waiting patiently will produce higher yields. If you prefer, you can cut the fruiting block at the base with a sharp knife. When storing Reishi, you can use a dehydrator to keep them dry.

Reishi mushrooms are a picky species, so the substrate is extremely important. It can't grow on coffee grounds, cardboard, or other nonwoody materials. It prefers hardwoods such as oak. Some growers also add oats and wheat bran to the substrate, which helps the mycelium flourish. Reishi mushrooms are found in forests, on dead trees, stumps, and logs.

After harvesting, place the logs in a shady and protected area. Ideally, they should receive one inch of rain per week. If the logs become too dry, you may need to provide irrigation. During the fruiting stage, Reishi mushrooms form conks. Harvesting them at this stage will yield a larger yield. Growers can cultivate Reishi mushrooms indoors or outdoors. Hardwood sawdust is the ideal growing medium for Reishi mushrooms.

Cultivating Reishi on Sawdust and Bran

If you don't have much time to wait, you can harvest Reishi mushrooms on sawdust or bran. The fruiting process can take between eight and twelve weeks. Alternatively, you can buy Reishi mushrooms online and harvest them fresh. Once you have harvested the Reishi mushrooms, you can dry them for use. These mushrooms are an excellent way to make a healthy, nutritious supplement for your body.

Here are the basic steps to grow Reishi on sawdust and bran:

1. Prepare the sawdust and bran mixture: Mix sawdust and bran in a 4:1 ratio by volume. The sawdust should be hardwood sawdust, such as Oak or maple. The bran can be wheat or rice bran. Moisten the mixture with water until it reaches 60-65% moisture content.

2. Sterilize the sawdust and bran mixture: Place the sawdust and bran mixture into autoclavable bags and sterilize them in a pressure cooker or autoclave at 15 psi for 1.5-2 hours. This will kill any bacteria or fungi present in the substrate.

3. Inoculate the sawdust and bran mixture: Allow the sawdust and bran mixture to cool to room temperature. Inoculate the bags with Reishi mushroom spawn by mixing the spawn into the sawdust and bran mixture. Seal the bags with a filter patch to allow for gas exchange.

4. Incubate the bags: Place the bags in a dark, warm location (between 20-27°C or 68-81°F) and allow them to incubate for 4-6 weeks until the mycelium fully colonizes the substrate.

5. Initiate fruiting: Once the bags are fully colonized, place them in a cooler location (around 15°C or 59°F) with high humidity (around 90%). Expose them to light for a few hours each day to stimulate fruiting.

6. Harvest: Reishi mushrooms can take several weeks to mature. They are typically harvested when the caps are fully developed and the edges start to turn upward.

7. Repeat the process: After harvesting, the bags can be sterilized again and reused for another round of cultivation.

Cultivating Reishi mushrooms on sawdust and bran requires careful diligence and sterile techniques. However, with proper care and maintenance, this method can yield a high-quality harvest of Reishi mushrooms.

Health Benefits of Reishi Mushrooms

Reishi mushrooms, also known as lingzhi mushrooms, are a type of edible and medicinal mushroom that have been used in traditional Chinese and Japanese medicine for centuries. Here are some of the potential health benefits of reishi mushrooms:

1. Boosts immune function: Reishi mushrooms contain beta-glucans and other polysaccharides that have been shown to stimulate the immune system. They may help improve the body's response to infections and diseases, as well as enhance the efficacy of vaccines.

2. Reduces inflammation: Reishi mushrooms contain compounds called triterpenoids, which have been shown to have anti-inflammatory effects. They may be beneficial for people with conditions characterized by chronic inflammation, such as arthritis, asthma, or inflammatory bowel disease.

3. May have anticancer properties: Some studies suggest that reishi mushrooms may have anticancer properties, as they contain compounds that have been shown to inhibit the growth of cancer cells and stimulate the immune system's response to cancer.

1. However, more research is needed to confirm these findings.

4. Improves liver function: Reishi mushrooms may help improve liver function by reducing oxidative stress and inflammation in the liver. They may be beneficial for people with liver disease or those who consume alcohol regularly.

5. Reduces stress and anxiety: Reishi mushrooms contain compounds that have been shown to have calming and stress-reducing effects. They may be beneficial for people with anxiety or stress-related disorders.

6. May improve sleep quality: Some studies suggest that reishi mushrooms may help improve sleep quality by reducing stress and anxiety and promoting relaxation.

They may be beneficial for people with sleep disorders or insomnia.

Overall, reishi mushrooms are a nutritious and potentially beneficial addition to a healthy diet. However, it's important to note that more research is needed to fully understand their health benefits and potential side effects. As with any supplement or dietary change, it's best to talk to a healthcare provider before incorporating reishi mushrooms into your diet.

CHAPTER SEVENTEEN:

Cultivating Chaga Mushrooms

Chaga Mushroom Growth Parameters

Chaga mushroom (Inonotus obliquus) is a medicinal mushroom that grows on birch trees in the northern hemisphere. It is highly valued for its potential health benefits, such as antioxidant, anti-inflammatory, and immune-boosting properties.

The growth of Chaga mushroom is influenced by various parameters, including:

1. Host Tree: Chaga mushroom grows exclusively on birch trees, with the primary hosts being yellow birch (Betula alleghaniensis) and white birch (Betula papyrifera). The health and vitality of the host tree are important for the growth and quality of the Chaga mushroom.

2. Geographic Location: Chaga mushroom grows in cold regions, such as northern Europe, Asia, and North America. The temperature, humidity, and sunlight exposure in a particular geographic location can affect the growth of Chaga mushroom.

3. Harvest Time: The ideal time to harvest Chaga mushroom is during the fall and winter months when it has fully matured and hardened on the host tree. Harvesting Chaga mushrooms during other times of the year may affect their quality and potency.

4. Extraction Method: The extraction method used to extract the beneficial compounds from Chaga mushrooms can affect their potency and quality. Common methods include hot water extraction, alcohol extraction, and dual extraction (hot water and alcohol).

5. Cultivation Conditions: Chaga mushrooms can also be cultivated under controlled

conditions in laboratories and indoor environments. Optimal conditions for cultivation include a pH range of 5.0-5.5, a temperature range of 18-25°C, and high humidity levels.

6. Nutrient Availability: Chaga mushroom requires certain nutrients to grow, such as glucose, fructose, and minerals like potassium, calcium, and magnesium. These nutrients can be obtained from the host tree or provided through artificial supplementation in cultivation settings.

Overall, the growth of Chaga mushrooms is influenced by various factors, and optimizing these parameters can help improve the quality and potency of the final product.

How to Cultivate Chaga Mushrooms on Live Trees

Cultivating Chaga mushrooms on live trees is a process that requires patience and careful attention to detail. Here are some steps you can follow to grow Chaga mushrooms on live trees:

1. Identify the right tree species: Chaga mushrooms grow on several tree species, including birch, maple, and elm. However, they are mostly found on birch trees. Look for healthy, mature trees with rough bark.

2. Find a suitable site: Choose a site with enough shade and moisture. Chaga mushrooms thrive in damp and humid environments.

3. Obtain Chaga mushroom spores: Chaga mushrooms can be grown from spores or through inoculation with a Chaga-infected birch tree. You can obtain spores from a reliable supplier or from a Chaga-infected tree.

4. Inoculate the tree: Drill a hole in the tree's bark and insert the Chaga mushroom

spores or a small piece of Chaga-infected bark into the hole. Cover the hole with wax or a bandage to prevent moisture loss.

5. Wait for the mushroom to grow: It may take several months or even years for the Chaga mushroom to grow. Monitor the tree regularly for any signs of growth or damage.

6. Harvest the mushroom: Once the mushroom has reached maturity, it can be harvested by carefully removing it from the tree with a sharp knife. Be sure to leave some Chaga on the tree to allow for future growth.

7. Dry and store the mushroom: After harvesting, dry the Chaga mushroom in a warm, dry place. Once it is completely dry, store it in an airtight container.

Remember, cultivating Chaga mushrooms on live trees requires careful attention and patience. It is important to ensure that the tree is healthy and that the environment is suitable for growth.

Chaga is a black conk found on white and yellow birch trees. The interior is yellow to brown and brittle. It is also known as the false tinder fungus because it has been used to create fire-starting material. Chaga is not poisonous and doesn't produce any harmful look-alikes.

When you're ready to start your project, you need to start by harvesting your first batch of chaga. You can use a hatchet to cut the fungus without damaging the tree. A small piece can last for several months and can be reused six times. Because Chaga is a polypore mass, it requires a long simmering time for its beneficial components to be absorbed by your body.

Chaga is a type of fungus found on broadleaf trees and causes sterile conks. It is known as "chaga" in Asia and in Finland. It is commonly grown for its medicinal properties, as it is not toxic and can help in many ways, including enhancing your immune system.

The birch tree is a prime location to grow Chaga mushrooms, The mushroom grows on birch trees, but it is not poisonous, and you can find them growing wild in cold climates. If you wish to cultivate Chaga, you should first plant at least 2 ha of birch trees. You can then propagate the mushrooms by inserting wooden dowels impregnated with mycelia into 5cm holes in the birch trees. The Chaga dowels should be planted three to five years apart. This is because the mushroom grows very slowly, so it will take longer to harvest the mushrooms than many others. However, if you have the patience, you will be rewarded with a delicious product.

After you've harvested the chaga, it's time to dry it. If you can find a sunny window, place the soaked pieces on it. You should leave them for three days. They should feel firm to the touch. Never dry chaga in the oven. Use a dehydrator at a temperature of 120 degrees Fahrenheit (49 degrees Celsius). After drying the Chaga, you can put it into a jar and keep it in the refrigerator for up to 3 days. You can also steep it in a liter of water to extract its flavor.

Chaga takes years to grow, so be sure to only pick a portion when it has reached about a grapefruit's size. Then, leave about one-third of the mushroom untouched. Don't cut into the tree unless you've made a firm plan. It's not uncommon to encounter an invasive species of fungus. Make sure to follow all safety guidelines when harvesting chaga and respect the tree's ecosystem.

Extracting Chaga's Beneficial Compounds

Chaga is a mushroom that is commonly known for its anti-inflammatory and immune-enhancing properties. This mushroom contains terpenes, which are nutrients extracted from its bark and tissues. These compounds help reduce inflammation in the body and are a significant contributor to Chaga's antimicrobial properties. Betulinic acid, a terpene in Chaga, is particularly useful for reducing the threat of bacteria, fungi, and viruses to the human body. Moreover, it has an inhibitory effect on the influenza virus and the HIV virus, two diseases that can be caused by the immune system.

Using HPLC-MS-MS (high-performance liquid chromatographymass spectrometry), researchers identified metabolites in aqueous extracts of French Chaga. They were able to compare the concentrations of these metabolites with those of traditional preparations of Chaga, such as powder, tincture, and decoction. The results showed that betulinic acid and inotodiol were particularly effective against cancer cells.

The most important thing to remember when cultivating chaga mushrooms is to avoid harvesting them from dead or dried trees. These mushrooms may be contaminated with harmful fungi. The best way to avoid mold on the Chaga mushroom is to dry them in a dry room and break them into small pieces. Always store your harvest in an airtight container away from direct sunlight. Whenever possible, avoid using a saw to cut the mushroom.

When you harvest chaga mushrooms, be sure to leave at least 20% of the fungus behind. This way, the Chaga will grow back. This practice is not only thoughtful but also selfish. If you harvest chaga mushrooms and leave the remaining 20%, you can return in a few years to collect more. This practice is not only illegal, but it gives the mushrooms an unfavorable public image.

Developing chaga mushrooms on several birch trees is not an impossible feat. The birch tree needs to be wounded and infected to support the fungus, which then multiplies and forms a mass known as chaga. The mushroom is not a fruiting part of the fungus but a dense mass of wood fiber and mycelium. In other words, the fungus must be growing on multiple birch trees to develop the best mushrooms.

The Chaga mushroom grows on a tree that is about 20 feet or 40 feet tall, so it's not likely to grow in the middle of a forest. However, you can harvest chaga from a single tree if you are willing to work a little. It's easier to harvest chaga when the conk is more than a grapefruit-sized mass. Remember to leave one-third of the mass unharvested, as cutting it can damage the tree. Remember, if you kill the tree, so will the Chaga that lives in it.

There are many ethical guidelines to follow when harvesting chaga. These include not cutting down trees or climbing up them, harvesting only what you need for the year, and not damaging the trees. It is also recommended that you leave some conks on the tree. This way, you can help the fungus grow back. Listed below are some of the ethical guidelines to follow when harvesting chaga.

Harvesting chaga from a dead or dry tree is not recommended. Chaga mushrooms grow in living trees, but if you are harvesting them from dead or dry trees, you will not be harvesting a high-quality mushroom. Similarly, if you are harvesting chaga from a live tree, the conks you collect will contain only a small portion of the mushroom.

One of the most common questions about this mushroom is whether it is edible or not. If you are trying to grow Chaga mushrooms, The Chaga and the host tree live together in symbiosis. The Chaga extends the life of the host tree so that the fungi can thrive. They are mainly found on birch trees, but they can also grow on other trees. In northern climes, they are plentiful and widespread. Birch trees grow at higher altitudes in forests. They thrive in cold, moist conditions and are known to be highly resistant to hard winters. You can also find Chaga mushrooms in Finland, Russia, Kazakhstan, South Korea, and even North America.

Health Benefits of Chaga Mushrooms

Chaga mushrooms have been used for centuries in traditional medicine to promote health and wellness. Here are some of the potential health benefits of consuming Chaga:

Antioxidant properties: Chaga mushrooms are rich in antioxidants, which can help protect the body against oxidative stress and free radicals.

1. Anti-inflammatory effects: Chaga mushrooms contain compounds that have been shown to have anti-inflammatory effects. This may help reduce inflammation in the body, which can contribute to chronic diseases.

2. Immune system support: Some studies suggest that Chaga mushrooms may help boost the immune system and improve immune function.

3. Anti-cancer properties: Chaga mushrooms contain betulinic acid, a compound that has been shown to have anti-cancer properties in some studies.

4. Lowering cholesterol: Chaga mushrooms may help lower cholesterol levels in the body, which can reduce the risk of heart disease.

5. Promoting liver health: Chaga mushrooms may help support liver health and improve liver function.

6. Managing diabetes: Some studies suggest that Chaga mushrooms may help improve blood sugar control and insulin sensitivity in people with diabetes.

7. It is important to note that while there is some evidence to support these health benefits, more research is needed to fully understand the effects of Chaga mushrooms on human health. Additionally, individuals should speak with their healthcare provider before using Chaga mushrooms for medicinal purposes, as they can interact with certain medications and may not be safe for everyone to consume.

Chapter Eighteen:

How to Cultivate Turkey Tails

Turkey Tail Growth Parameters

Turkey tail (Trametes versicolor) is a type of medicinal mushroom that grows commonly on dead wood in forests around the world. Here are some of the growth parameters that are important to consider when cultivating turkey tail:

1. Substrate: Turkey tail mushrooms grow on a variety of wood-based substrates, including hardwood sawdust, wood chips, and logs. The substrate should be prepared by pasteurizing or sterilizing it to prevent contamination by other fungi or bacteria.

2. Temperature: Turkey tail mushrooms grow best at temperatures between 20-30°C (68-86°F). It is important to maintain a consistent temperature throughout the growth cycle.

3. Humidity: Turkey tail mushrooms require high humidity levels, between 80-90%, to grow properly. This can be achieved through misting or using a humidifier.

4. Light: Turkey tail mushrooms do not require light to grow, but they can benefit from indirect light during the fruiting stage.

5. Air exchange: Adequate air exchange is important for the growth and development of turkey tail mushrooms. This can be achieved through ventilation or using an air pump.

6. Spawn inoculation: Turkey tail mushrooms can be grown using spawn inoculation, where a small amount of mycelium is added to the substrate. The mycelium will then grow and colonize the substrate, eventually producing fruiting bodies.

7. Fruiting: Turkey tail mushrooms typically begin fruiting 3-6 months after inoculation, depending on the growth conditions. Fruiting can be induced by reducing the temperature and increasing air exchange.

By carefully controlling these growth parameters, it is possible to successfully cultivate turkey tail mushrooms and harness their powerful medicinal properties.

Cultivating Turkey Tails on Logs

1. Cut 3"-6" hardwood trees between December and March to 3'4' length. Remove all branches and make sure the bark is intact without being damaged and free of fungus and contamination.

2. Cut with an 8mm drill bit or 5/16inch drill bit, drill 1" deep holes 6" apart and 2" between holes in each row

3. Fill holes with either dowels or sawdust. When using dowels, you may either use spiral grooved (pictured) or straight grooved, and metric size 8mmx25mm or standard 5/16inch x 1inch. Both types of dowels work well for growing mushroom plug spawn and can be used either with either an 8mm drill bit or a 5/16 inch drill bit. Each dowel is hammered in until it is flush with the surface of the log. If you are using sawdust spawn, you will need to use an inoculation tool. Make sure that the hole is completely full of sawdust.

4. Finally, cover each inoculated hole with wax to protect the spawn from drying out, being eaten by insects, and keeping contamination spores from entering the logs.

5. Stack the logs in a shaded environment under conifer trees is ideal, or you can use 40-60% shade cloth if you do not have a tree canopy.

To ensure the success of your mushroom cultivation, you need to properly prepare your logs for inoculation. Ideally, the logs should have six inches between holes, spaced two or three inches apart on the circumference. After you have prepared the logs, place the mushroom spawn inside the holes. After the mushroom spawn has been placed, you can seal the holes with melted wax to keep out insects and other competing fungi.

To start growing Turkey Tail mushrooms, you will need a large space and plenty of sunlight. Turkey tail mushrooms are known to be hardy and require a large amount of sunlight. You will need at least four square meters for your mushroom cultivation. You will also need logs with a diameter of approximately two feet and a depth of three inches. Turkey tail mushrooms are edible and contain several active ingredients, including beta-glucans. These polysaccharides have anti-tumor and anti-viral properties.

For centuries, Turkey tail has been used in traditional Chinese medicine as a powerful immune system potentiator. It grows wild on tree trunks and logs of both living and dead trees. This species is small and thin, fleshed with pores instead of gills. Turkey tails grow in temperate climates all over the world. If you are interested in harvesting turkey tail mushrooms, you can try a variety of methods to grow them in your own backyard.

To harvest turkey tails, you can inoculate sawdust or logs with mycelium. In several weeks, the mycelium of the Turkey Tail will have colonized the block. By then, the turkey tail will be dense and white on the surface. You will know you've harvested turkey tails when the sawdust blocks are thick and white.

Turkey Tail mushrooms grow best on decayed and dead wood. This mushroom can grow on about seventy types of hardwood in the U.S. and is also capable of thriving on coniferous trees. This mushroom spreads by depositing its spores into fallen wood. In addition to trees, the mushroom can colonize dead stumps and stressed living trees. In this way, cultivating the mushroom on logs and sawdust has numerous benefits.

The best time to grow turkey tails is in the fall or winter months when the fungus releases spores. It reproduces rapidly, so cultivating the mushroom at this time can ensure you have plenty of fresh mushrooms. Look for the characteristic pore surface - it should resemble the shape of a turkey tail. To distinguish it from other mushrooms, select specimens with white or cream rings on the conk's edge. The pores on the cap are small and do not cover the entire surface. Turkey tails grow and dry up in about one season, and the resulting mushroom is edible but not poisonous.

One of the easiest mushrooms to grow at home is turkey tails. These multicolored polypore mushrooms are easy to grow, require little care, and produce high-quality medicinal tinctures and teas.

To grow turkey tails, you will need sawdust or logs and a dark location that stays between 18 and 24 C. To grow a turkey tail, inoculate the sawdust block with the fungus, and wait a couple of weeks. The sawdust block should colonize in two to three weeks. An additional week may be necessary to allow fruiting.

How to Cultivate Turkey Tails on Sawdust and Bran

Cultivating turkey tail mushrooms on sawdust and bran is a process that requires some equipment and specific steps. Here are some steps you can follow to grow turkey tail mushrooms on sawdust and bran:

1. Prepare the substrate: In a large pot, mix together sawdust and bran in a ratio of 5:1. You can use hardwood sawdust or a mix of hardwood and softwood sawdust. Pour enough water over the mixture to make it moist but not soaking wet.

2. Sterilize the substrate: To prevent contamination, you need to sterilize the substrate. Place the mixture into sterilization bags and seal them. You can sterilize the bags by using a pressure cooker or a steam sterilizer. Follow the instructions provided with the sterilizer to ensure proper sterilization.

3. Inoculate the substrate: Once the substrate has been sterilized, let it cool down to room temperature. Then, add turkey tail mushroom spawn to the bags. You can purchase the spawn from a reputable supplier. Mix the spawn well into the substrate.

4. Incubate the bags: Place the inoculated bags in a warm, dark place with good ventilation. The ideal temperature for incubation is between 65-75°F. Depending on the temperature and humidity, it may take 2-4 weeks for the mycelium to colonize the substrate.

5. Prepare the fruiting chamber: Once the mycelium has colonized the substrate, it is time to prepare the fruiting chamber. You can use plastic storage containers or large plastic bags. Make sure the container or bag has air holes for ventilation.

6. Transfer the substrate: Cut several holes in the sterilization bags and transfer the substrate into the fruiting chamber. Make sure the substrate is level and spread evenly.

7. Maintain humidity: Spray the substrate with water to maintain humidity. The ideal humidity range is between 85-95%. You can also cover the container or bag with a plastic sheet to maintain humidity.

8. Harvest the mushrooms: Turkey tail mushrooms will begin to appear after 2-3 weeks. Harvest them by cutting them off with a sharp knife. Leave some of the mushrooms on the substrate to allow for future growth.

Remember, cultivating turkey tail mushrooms on sawdust and bran requires careful attention and proper sterilization techniques. It is important to ensure the substrate and fruiting chamber are clean and free of contaminants.

Sawdust should be at least 10% ash and one-half percent wheat or oat bran. The combination of bran and sawdust will boost spawn growth and reduce contamination. Sawdust and bran should be mixed to a ratio of 10 to 20 percent before water is added. Sawdust blocks with bran and grain spawn should contain a higher proportion of sawdust than bran.

Turkey Tail mushrooms do well on oak sawdust. They also grow well on maple, beech, and ironwood sawdust. Turkey Tails mushrooms prefer a medium that is moist and bumpy.

Turkey Tail Health Benefits

Turkey tail (Trametes versicolor) is a type of medicinal mushroom that has been used for centuries in traditional Chinese medicine and other cultures around the world. Here are some of the potential health benefits of turkey tail:

1. Immune system support: Turkey tail contains polysaccharides and beta-glucans that have been shown to boost the immune system by increasing the activity of natural killer cells and other immune cells.

2. Anti-inflammatory properties: The polysaccharides and other compounds in turkey tail have anti-inflammatory effects, which may help to reduce inflammation in the body and improve conditions such as arthritis and inflammatory bowel disease.

3. Anti-cancer properties: Turkey tail contains compounds such as polysaccharides, peptides and triterpenoids that have been shown to have anti-cancer effects, particularly in breast cancer and colorectal cancer.

4. Gut health: Turkey tail contains prebiotic compounds that can help to support a healthy gut microbiome, which is important for overall health and immunity.

5. Antioxidant properties: Turkey tail contains antioxidants such as phenols and flavonoids, which can help to protect the body against oxidative stress and damage from free radicals.

6. Respiratory health: Turkey tail has been used in traditional medicine to treat respiratory conditions such as bronchitis and asthma, and preliminary research suggests that it may have beneficial effects on lung function.

7. Cognitive function: Some studies suggest that turkey tail may have cognitive-enhancing effects, potentially due to its antioxidant and anti-inflammatory properties.

Overall, turkey tail is a promising medicinal mushroom with a wide range of potential health benefits. However, more research is needed to fully understand its effects and mechanisms of action.

CHAPTER NINETEEN:

How to Cultivate Lion's Mane Mushrooms

Growth Parameters of Lion's Mane Mushrooms

Lion's mane mushrooms (Hericium erinaceus) have specific growth parameters that can influence their growth and yield. Here are some key factors that can affect the growth of lion's mane mushrooms:

1. Temperature: Lion's mane mushrooms prefer cooler temperatures between 55-65°F (13-18°C) for optimal growth. Higher temperatures can inhibit their growth and reduce their yield.

2. Humidity: Lion's mane mushrooms require high humidity levels between 80-90% to grow successfully. You can maintain humidity levels by misting the substrate with water or by using a humidifier.

3. Light: Lion's mane mushrooms do not require light to grow, but they do need indirect light for the mycelium to develop properly. They can grow in low light conditions or in complete darkness.

4. Substrate: Lion's mane mushrooms can grow on a variety of substrates, including sawdust, straw, and hardwood logs. The substrate should be sterilized to prevent contamination and should be supplemented with nutrients like soybean meal, rice bran, or wheat bran.

5. Spawn ratio: The spawn ratio refers to the amount of mushroom spawn to the substrate. The ideal spawn ratio for lion's mane mushrooms is 5-10% by weight. Adding too much spawn can lead to overcrowding and slow down the growth of the mushrooms.

6. Harvesting: Lion's mane mushrooms can be harvested when they reach maturity, which is typically 3-5 months after inoculation. Harvesting can be done by cutting the fruiting body off the substrate with a sharp knife.

Remember, lion's mane mushrooms require specific growth parameters to thrive. Monitoring and controlling these parameters can help ensure a successful harvest.

How To Cultivate Lions Mane on Logs

Growing lion's mane mushrooms on logs is a popular method of cultivation, especially for those who prefer a more natural and sustainable approach. Here are the steps to grow lion's mane mushrooms on logs:

1. Choose logs: Select fresh hardwood logs, preferably from trees such as oak, maple, or beech, which are between 3-8 inches in diameter and 3-4 feet long. Avoid using logs that have been recently cut, as they may contain harmful chemicals or resins.

2. Inoculate the logs: Drill 5/16-inch holes into the logs, spaced about 23 inches apart in rows that are 2-3 inches apart. Then, insert plugs of lion's mane mushroom spawn into the holes. You can purchase the spawn from a reputable supplier. Seal the holes with wax to prevent contamination.

3. Store the logs: Place the inoculated logs in a shady and humid location, such as under a tree or in a forest. Keep them off the ground to prevent rotting. Stack the logs in a crisscross pattern to allow air circulation.

4. Water the logs: Water the logs regularly to keep them moist but not soaking wet. The ideal moisture level is around 40-60%. You can use a spray bottle or a sprinkler to water the logs.

5. Wait for the mushrooms to grow: Lion's mane mushrooms take between 6-18 months to fully colonize the logs, depending on the environmental conditions. When the mushrooms start to appear, mist them with water regularly to maintain humidity levels.

6. Harvest the mushrooms: Lion's mane mushrooms are ready to harvest when they reach maturity, which is typically around 6-12 months after inoculation. Gently twist the mushrooms to remove them from the log or cut them off with a sharp knife.

Remember, growing lion's mane mushrooms on logs requires patience and careful attention to environmental conditions. It may take several months to a year for the mushrooms to grow, but the result is a sustainable and natural source of delicious and nutritious mushrooms.

Among the most common methods to grow lion's mane mushrooms on logs and sawdust is inoculating the logs with mushroom spawn. Once the logs are inoculated with spawn, you need to monitor the colonization process.

To inoculate logs with Lions' Mane mushrooms, you will need a sugar maple, American beech, or other soft hardwood logs. Cutting trees between January and October is ideal, as temperatures are 50 degrees or higher. For most types of logs, you will need around 2030 plugs per log.

The best type of wood to use for inoculation is oak, maple, or birch, though a few other types, such as poplar, willow, and black walnut, will also work. The easiest logs to work with are three feet long. Inoculating your logs is best done in the spring or fall because they are cooler than in the summer.

You will notice the first signs of colonization after the third day. The mycelium will begin to spread out with long tendrils and white threads. These are the mushrooms' roots. Shake the bucket often and check the mycelium for any signs of green mold or white threads. If you notice them, you are ready to harvest your mushrooms. You will see that your first flush of mushrooms may be small but that they'll quickly begin to fruit again.

Lion's Mane mushrooms do not require a lot of maintenance and will produce a harvest every year. Once inoculated in spring, logs can produce mushrooms by fall. To grow a more productive log, cut it longer than the logs used for growing other species. If you do not have wood available, you can buy a log that is longer than the logs used for mushroom cultivation. If you are not willing to cut your logs yourself, you can also buy spawn and inoculate logs with the mushrooms.

How To Cultivate Lions Mane Mushrooms on Sawdust and Bran

Cultivating lion's mane mushrooms on sawdust and bran is a simple and efficient way to grow this delicious and nutritious mushroom. Here are the steps to cultivate lion's mane mushrooms on sawdust and bran:

1. Gather the ingredients: You will need sawdust, bran, water, and lion's mane mushroom spawn. The sawdust should be fresh and untreated, and the bran should be wheat or rice bran.

2. Mix the ingredients: In a large pot, mix 5 parts sawdust, 2 parts bran, and 2 parts water. Heat the mixture over low heat, stirring occasionally, until it reaches a temperature of 160-180°F (71-82°C). This will pasteurize the mixture and kill off any harmful bacteria or fungi.

3. Cool the mixture: Let the mixture cool to room temperature, then add the lion's

mane mushroom spawn. The spawn should be added at a ratio of 5-10% by weight. Mix the spawn thoroughly into the sawdust and bran mixture.

4. Pack the mixture into containers: Pack the sawdust and bran mixture tightly into containers, such as plastic bags or jars. Leave some space at the top of the container to allow for the mushrooms to grow.

5. Incubate the containers: Place the containers in a dark and humid location, such as a closet or basement, and maintain a temperature of 70-75°F (21-24°C) and humidity of 80-90%. The mycelium will grow and colonize the substrate over the next 2-4 weeks.

6. Introduce fresh air: After the mycelium has colonized the substrate, poke several small holes in the containers to allow fresh air to circulate. This will trigger the growth of the fruiting bodies.

7. Maintain humidity: Continue to maintain high humidity levels by misting the substrate regularly. The fruiting bodies will start to form within 2-4 weeks.

8. Harvest the mushrooms: The lion's mane mushrooms are ready to harvest when they reach maturity, which is typically around 3-4 weeks after the fruiting bodies start to form. Gently twist the mushrooms to remove them from the substrate.

Remember, cultivating lion's mane mushrooms on sawdust and bran requires careful attention to environmental conditions, especially temperature and humidity. With proper care, you can enjoy a bountiful harvest of delicious and nutritious mushrooms.

If you have ever wanted to grow your own lion's mane mushrooms, you will have to be patient. This species of mushroom can take quite a while to fruit. The wait is worth it, however.

You can obtain logs and sawdust from a landscaping company or from a tree surgeon. If you cannot get wood chips, wood pellets are an easy, inexpensive, and convenient alternative. You can purchase wood pellets online or locally. Make sure you purchase hardwood pellets, as these will grow lion's mane mushrooms the best. Despite its name, all hardwoods are perfect for growing lion's mane mushrooms, so you can get the best results from your efforts by combining the two.

To harvest your lion's mane mushrooms, you should pick them before they turn brown or when they have formed clear teeth. If you can, cut them as close to the base as possible, and be sure not to damage their spines. You can also soak the logs in water and store them in the refrigerator for up to two weeks. Just remember to check on them regularly to make sure they do not develop mold.

Nutrient supplements for growing lion's mane mushrooms For optimal growth of Lion's Mane mushrooms, hardwood sawdust supplemented with soy hulls is recommended. You can also use the master's mix, which is a mixture of hardwood sawdust and soy hulls, hydrated to 60 percent. Straw is another inexpensive substrate, but wood-based substrates are more reliable.

Lion's Mane is difficult to find in grocery stores, but you can purchase spores from specialty mushroom growers and start growing at home.

You can buy mushroom starter kits that contain a variety of supplements, including vitamins A and D. A good source of these vitamins is sawdust, as it can provide the nutrients that your mushrooms need. Also, be sure to buy a compost-based mushroom starter mix. It will give you a healthier crop in less time. When grown on sawdust and bran, lion's mane mushrooms have the ability to grow in containers, a process that makes growing a healthy mushroom easier.

Lion's Mane is an easy mushroom to grow, but you must follow a few steps to make it a fruit. To prevent this, start with a liquid culture and cut "x's" in the bottom of the blocks where the fruit is forming. Pins will continue to grow until they become large mushrooms outside the bag.

Health Benefits of Lions Mane Mushrooms

Lion's mane mushrooms have been used for centuries in traditional Chinese medicine to promote overall health and wellbeing. Recent scientific research has also uncovered several potential health benefits of lion's mane mushrooms, including:

1. Improved cognitive function: Lion's mane mushrooms contain compounds called hericenones and erinacines, which have been shown to stimulate the growth of nerve cells and improve cognitive function. Several studies have found that lion's mane mushrooms may help improve memory, concentration, and focus.

2. Reduced inflammation: Lion's mane mushrooms contain antioxidants and anti-inflammatory compounds that may help reduce inflammation throughout the body. Chronic inflammation has been linked to a number of health problems, including heart disease, cancer, and Alzheimer's disease.

3. Boosted immune function: Lion's mane mushrooms contain beta-glucans, which are complex sugars that have been shown to stimulate the immune system and

help the body fight off infections and diseases.

4.   Lowered risk of heart disease: The antioxidants and anti-inflammatory compounds in lion's mane mushrooms may also help reduce the risk of heart disease by improving cholesterol levels and reducing oxidative stress.

5.   Improved digestive health: Lion's mane mushrooms contain dietary fiber and other compounds that may help improve digestive health by promoting the growth of beneficial gut bacteria and reducing inflammation in the gut.

6.   Potential anti-cancer effects: Some preliminary studies have suggested that lion's mane mushrooms may have anti-cancer effects by inhibiting the growth and spread of cancer cells. However, more research is needed to confirm these findings.

Overall, lion's mane mushrooms are a nutritious and tasty addition to any diet and may provide a range of potential health benefits. However, it's important to note that more research is needed to fully understand the effects of lion's mane mushrooms on human health.

CHAPTER TWENTY:

Cultivating Psilocybin Mushrooms

Psilocybin Mushroom Growth Parameters

Psilocybin mushrooms, also known as "magic mushrooms," are a type of fungi that contain the psychoactive compound psilocybin. If you are interested in growing psilocybin mushrooms, here are some important growth parameters to consider:

1. Substrate: Psilocybin mushrooms grow on a substrate, which is the material that the mushrooms consume as they grow. Common substrates for psilocybin mushrooms include brown rice flour, vermiculite, and sawdust.

2. Temperature: Psilocybin mushrooms prefer to grow in a temperature range of 20-27°C (68-81°F).

3. Humidity: Psilocybin mushrooms require high humidity levels in order to grow. Ideally, the humidity level should be between 90-95%.

4. Light: Psilocybin mushrooms do not require light to grow, but they will not grow in complete darkness. It's best to provide them with indirect light, such as the light from a nearby window.

5. Air exchange: Psilocybin mushrooms require fresh air exchange to grow properly. This can be accomplished by opening the lid of the container they are growing in for a few minutes each day or by using a small fan to circulate air.

6. pH level: Psilocybin mushrooms prefer a pH level between 5.5-7.5.

7. Sterility: It's important to maintain a sterile environment when growing psilocybin mushrooms. This can be achieved by using sterile equipment and a clean work area and by sterilizing the substrate before use.

Keep in mind that growing psilocybin mushrooms is illegal in many countries and can be dangerous if not done properly. It's important to do thorough research and follow safety guidelines before attempting to grow psilocybin mushrooms.

PF Tek (Psilocybin Fanaticus)

PF Tek is a substrate used for growing psychedelic mushrooms. It contains a high-quality mix of nutrients, which helps to create dense colonies of spawn.

Basic recipe for Substrate for PF Tek:

- Two-parts vermiculite
- One-part brown rice flour
- One-part water

Other needed materials:

- Spore syringe

- Half-pint canning jars

- Aluminum foil

- Large pot or pressure cooker hammer and nail

- Flame source

- Plastic tub fruiting chamber

- Incubation area

- Clean workspace

Instructions:

1. The first step in this process is mixing the vermiculite and water. Make sure the vermiculite is fully saturated. Let add the brown rice flour and mix until the vermiculite is fully coated

2. The next step is to fill and cap the jars. Fill the jars with substrate leaving ½" of space on the top. Do not tap down the substrate using a hammer and nail to poke four holes in the edges of the lids. Make sure the holes are larger than the tip of the syringe. Cap the filled jars the cover each jar with aluminum foil

3. Then you sterilize the jars and their contents by giving them to boiling in a pot for 1 ½ hours or using a pressure cooker for 45 minutes at 15 psi

4. The next step is inoculating the substrate. When the jars are completely cooled, sterilize the spore syringe by heating the tip in a red-hot flame, allowing it to cool, and then inject the spore's solution into each jar through each hole.

5. Next, you need to set jars in a warm dark place to incubate so the mycelium can completely colonize.

6. Remove the cakes from the jars.

7. When each cake is out, rinse, then soak in cold water for 24 hours, then roll the cake in dry vermiculite (soaking stimulates fruiting).

8. Place cakes into the fruiting chamber. Be careful to give each cake adequate space and monitor temperature and humidity very closely.

9. Harvest mushrooms by twisting and pulling. Remove all the mushrooms completely then, you can start a new fruiting cycle.

Inoculation, which involves injecting the spores into the substrate. The spores will develop into mycelium and gradually colonize the substrate. A spore syringe contains 10 to 20 ml of spore solution, which is enough for about ten to twenty substrate jars. Use gloves to avoid contamination. The needle of the spore syringe should be red hot.

The PF Tek cultivation manual recommends using four 240-ml jars for the mushroom cultivation process. These jars can easily colonize and contain enough nutrients for multiple flushes. Using larger jars is not recommended as the jars are more prone to contamination. To use PF Tek for growing psychedelic mushrooms, make sure to follow the instruction manual thoroughly.

Uncle Ben's Tek

One of the easiest ways to grow psilocybin mushrooms is by using Uncle Ben's Tek. This is a simple and inexpensive method that will grow 3 ounces of dry mushrooms for under $12. If you're not a biochemist, this method is perfect for beginners. It's also easy to find, which makes it a good choice for those with limited budgets.

First, you need to purchase some spores and liquid culture in syringes. You must sterilize all tools and materials before beginning to grow your psilocybin mushrooms. You don't need a pressure cooker; you can simply use rice bags. Make sure to sterilize your spore syringe and the needle. Once you've sterilized your spore syringe, you're ready to start inoculating the bags. For a successful 'Tek', you need the following materials: mushroom spores and instant brown rice (instant brown is the best).

How to do Uncle Bens Tek:

1. Massage bag gently and break up any clumps
2. Disinfect work area and yourself as well.
3. Wipe bag thoroughly with isopropanol and a rag.
4. Snip off corner of the bag.
5. Flame sterilize syringe tip.
6. Inject 1cc of liquid into bag through the slit corner
7. Place micropore tape over the hole making sure the hole is open before covering it. This allows the culture to breathe. Let the bags colonize, keeping them at room temperature or slightly cooler to slow the risk of contamination. When the bags are 30% colonized massage bags and break-up chunks.

Allow bags to colonize, and keep them at room temperature or slightly below cooler temperature slow the rate of contamination. When the bags are fully colonized, open bags to fruit them. You can add some coo-coir to case the mushrooms for larger yields or use the mycelium to inoculate bulk substrate.

A dehydrator is ideal for growing psychedelic mushrooms, and an airdrying sushi mat is useful. In addition, you'll need instant brown rice, which you can buy at a homewares store or catering supplier. Try to buy 10 bags at a time if possible. A small space heater (less than 80 deg F) will help maintain the proper temperature.

Once the mushrooms have reached a desired size, you can proceed to harvest them and a dehydrator or airdrying sushi mat. For the rice, you can use any variety of psilocybin cubensis

There are several ways to grow psilocybin mushrooms. One of the easiest and simplest is Uncle Ben's Tek. This method is ideal for beginners and can work with most types of Psilocybin cubensis strains. You can purchase the ingredients in bulk and combine them with any other bulk substrate method. This recipe is simple, affordable, and easy to follow.

There are a few steps to follow when you want to grow psilocybin mushrooms, and here are a few tips. First, you can use moist perlite to maintain the right humidity level. As fungi, mushrooms need both oxygen and CO_2, but CO_2 is heavier than air. Another step is to use a heating pad or a light. During the growing process, mushrooms need regular fresh air, and it is best to lift the lid of the container at least twice a day.

Constructing a Monotub

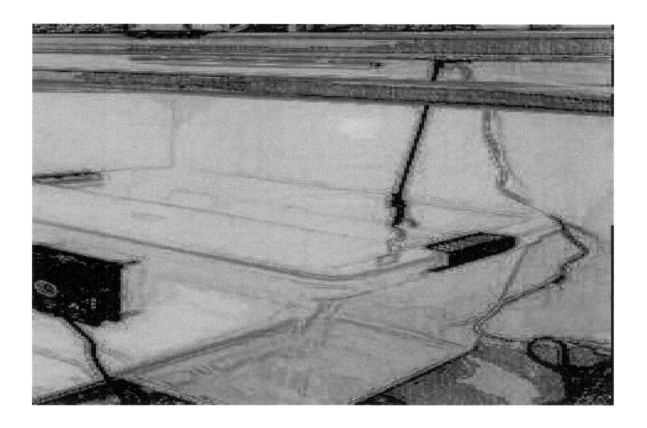

The temperature needs of the mushroom substrate are different for each type. A mushroom's substrate needs to be between 60 and 90 degrees Fahrenheit to grow its fruiting body. Any higher or lower than this will desiccate the mycelium and stymie its growth. Also, make sure that the temperature is not too low or too high. To grow mushrooms in a monotub, you will need to prepare the growing medium.

It can be made of coco coir, Hardwood sawdust, or even vermiculite. You may also need to use perlite. You can find these materials at any gardening store. You can also purchase them online. Listed below are the steps you need to take to create your own monotub.

A mono tub is an important part of mushroom cultivation. A monotub is a plastic tote modified with air holes Mostly used to cultivate psilocybin mushrooms, but I have cultivated several varieties of mushrooms using this method.

Material List:

- Transparent plastic bin with lid

- Black spray paint or black plastic

- Drill with a 2" hole saw

- Micropore tape and polyfill insulation

- Duct tape

Construction:

Paint the bottom of the tub. Paint up to the level you are adding substrate, or line the bottom with black plastic. This is important to block light keeping mushrooms from growing on the sides. Drill one 2" hole every 8" of length just above the paint or liner level, then fill the hole with polyfill insulations and use duct tape to keep it in place or use micropore tape instead to cover holes. This allows the substrate to breathe.

The monotub should be kept between 68 and 72 degrees Fahrenheit to encourage fruiting. To harvest mushrooms, simply twist and pull the bottom of the stem to release the hyphae pins. Once harvested, the monotub should be well-maintained to encourage several flushes of growth. The mycelium soil is recycled to garden soil, which provides additional nutrients and moisture.

Coco-coir substrate recipe

Easy Bulk Substrate Preparation Instructions

Materials:

- 1 Brick of Coco-Coir (Tip: If you want to make your life a little easier use Pre-Shredded Coir)

- 2 Quarts of Vermiculite

- 1 cup of Gypsum– This ingredient is optional but provides calcium and sulfur, which is needed for healthy mycelium growth and act as a pH buffer.

- 5 Gallon Bucket with Lid – Find this at hardware stores and building supplies
- 4 Quarts (one gallon) of Boiling Water. Tap water is fine; filtered water is better.

Instructions:

1. Place the coco coir into a five-gallon bucket. When using compressed coir bricks, it helps with hydration to break up the brick into smaller pieces.
2. Add 2 quarts of vermiculite to the 5-gallon bucket.
3. Place a large pot on the stove and add 4 quarts of water. Turn the burner to high and add gypsum to the water. Wait for the water to a boil.
4. Remove the pot from the heat and stir the gypsum/water mix using a large spoon, then pour the hot water over the ingredients in the five-gallon bucket.
5. Place the lid on the bucket and allow it to sit for 10 minutes. Once 10 minutes is up, remove the lid and stir up all the ingredients using a large spoon. Be careful, the substrate will be very hot, and steam will be released once the lid is opened.
6. Place the lid back on the bucket and allow the substrate to cool (46 hrs.).
7. When sufficiently cooled, it can be inoculated with mushroom spawn

After the coco-coir substrate is prepared, add a thin layer of grain spawn. Lay this layer in a lasagna-like pattern on top of the coco substrate mix. Make sure to enclose all the grains. These grains are nutrient-dense and pose a risk of contamination. Hence, they must be placed on top of the coco-substrate mix before mushroom cultivation.

Coco coir is a natural product made from coconut fiber. It has been increasingly popular as a hydroponic medium thanks to its affordability and ease of use. It is readily available in several forms - compressed, chipped, and ground - and is used for mushroom cultivation. The substrate provides proper drainage and helps mushrooms grow and produce thick, fleshy fruiting bodies. If you can't find coco coir, you can purchase it at local garden centers or online. Afterwards, you should soak coco coir in water until it becomes soft enough to handle the moisture coco-coir substrate is a mixture of coco coir and vermiculite. Coco coir contains some nutrients, while vermiculite is nutritionally inert. Both materials can retain water. A typical coco-coir and vermiculite mix is 1:1. Although it is not particularly nutritious for plants, coco-coir and vermiculite are both sufficient substrates for most types of mushroom cultivation. When choosing a coco-coir-vermiculite mix, it is important to make sure that the material is pasteurized, as they can absorb more water and become a more compact substrate.

While using coco coir as substrates for mushrooms will increase yield, it will not be the most effective option for all types of mushroom cultivation. Its low pH value and low absorption properties will limit the growth of fungi and bacteria. Coco-coir substrates are often mixed with aged manure to enrich the mushroom compost or gourmet mushroom mulch. The two materials are then left to partially decompose and added to the mushroom compost.

Using coco coir and vermiculite for mushroom cultivation is easy and affordable. Many people use coconut coir in monotubs and shotgun fruiting chambers. However, it is possible to use vermiculite, gypsum, and straw for their mushroom cultivation. In addition to coco coir and vermiculite, you can also use other materials like straw and manure.

Growing Wood Loving Psilocybin Outside on Wood Chips

Growing wood-loving psilocybin mushrooms outside on wood chips can be a more natural and sustainable method than indoor cultivation. However, it can also be more challenging and requires careful attention to environmental factors. Here are the basic steps:

1. Prepare the substrate: Wood chips are typically used as the substrate for outdoor cultivation of wood-loving psilocybin mushrooms. The wood chips should be clean and free of contaminants. Soak the wood chips in water overnight, then drain and

pasteurize them by heating them to 140-160°F for several hours.

2. Inoculate the substrate: Once the substrate has cooled down, it can be inoculated with spawn or colonized grains. The spawn can be spread evenly throughout the substrate, and then the entire mixture should be placed in a large container or bag, sealed, and left in a warm and dark location for several weeks.

3. Prepare the outdoor bed: Choose a shaded location with well-draining soil and no direct sunlight. Dig a hole or trench and layer the bottom with gravel or stones for drainage. Add a layer of cardboard or newspaper to prevent weeds from growing through the bed, then add the inoculated wood chips, and cover them with a layer of straw or leaves to retain moisture.

4. Monitor the bed: Water the bed regularly to keep it moist but not waterlogged. Check the bed regularly for signs of contamination or pests and remove any contaminated or dead material.

5. Harvest the mushrooms: The mushrooms will start to grow after several weeks, depending on the species and environmental conditions. Harvest the mushrooms by gently twisting and pulling them from the substrate when the caps have fully opened and the veils have broken.

6. Outdoor cultivation of psilocybin mushrooms is illegal in many parts of the world and may carry legal and safety risks. It's important to educate yourself on local laws and regulations and to ensure safe and responsible consumption.

Health Benefits of Psilocybin Mushrooms

Psilocybin Mushroom extract has been used to treat depression in patients. It has shown significant improvement in their psychological, emotional, and spiritual wellbeing. It can be an excellent remedy for people suffering from various kinds of mental disorders, such as anxiety and addiction. Here are some of the other benefits of psilocybin. In addition to treating depression, psilocybin can also be effective for patients with anxiety.

A modern-day psychedelic renaissance is underway for magic mushrooms. As misinformation about psychedelics fades, researchers are looking into the potential benefits and risks of psilocybin mushrooms. To learn more about the benefits of psilocybin, read on! In a recent study, researchers at the John Hopkins University administered three doses of psilocybin to smokers.

Currently, psilocybin is illegal in the state of Colorado and federally. However, recent landmark decriminalization in Denver has inspired similar reforms in other U.S. cities. Mycophiles are celebrating the historic change and are tired of being harassed for their use. They hope that this new law will help them become more open about their use.

While psilocybin has not been approved for clinical use under the Controlled Drugs and Substances Act, the study found that it may reduce symptoms of depression and anxiety in healthy individuals. Furthermore, the substance decreased symptoms of addiction and is believed to be a promising treatment for both anxiety and depression. Despite being illegal in the U.S., it has been proven to be effective in many trials.

Oregon and California are among the many states that are trying to make psilocybin mushrooms legal. One of the bills proposed in Iowa would remove psilocybin mushrooms from the state's list of controlled substances and legalize the substance for medical use only. California and Oregon are also considering similar legislative changes. Many people believe that the mushrooms are effective for treating depression, anxiety, and nicotine addiction.

A study published in the journal Psychopharmacology suggests that treatment for depression with Psilocybin mushroom extract can improve the quality of life for some depressed people. The study involved 24 people with moderate to severe depression. Most had previously tried standard antidepressants, and more than half of the participants had used them during their current episodes. Researchers note that the results of this study might be skewed because the participants knew that they were going to be given the drug.

The study compared the effects of psilocybin on blood flow in different parts of the brain. The amount of oxygenated blood flowing through the brain reflects how active certain regions of the brain are. Participants in the study underwent fMRI scans before and after the therapy, and they also completed an inventory to measure their depression symptoms. This was the first study of its kind to prove that psilocybin mushrooms can improve depression.

Research shows that psilocybin mushrooms can help with anxiety and depression, particularly when used with other therapies. It has traditionally been studied for its ability to relieve fears and anxiety in patients suffering from cancer and for its effectiveness in reducing symptoms of emotional trauma. Although the psychedelic effects are still in the early stages, some scientists believe that psilocybin may have a positive impact on substance abuse and anxiety.

While most people who try psychedelic drugs do so on their own, psilocybin is the most studied and most promising. It can help with anxiety, depression, and other mental health conditions. The mushroom's active ingredient, psilocybin, has been studied extensively in labs and clinical settings, and it is becoming increasingly popular among consumers and scientists alike. However, psilocybin is still illegal in most states.

How to Micro-Dose Psilocybin Mushrooms

Microdosing psilocybin mushrooms involves taking a sub-perceptual dose of the mushroom, which is typically about 0.1-0.5 grams of dried mushroom.

Here are the general steps to microdose psilocybin mushrooms:

1. Start with a reliable source of mushrooms: Ensure that you have a trustworthy source of psilocybin mushrooms that are correctly identified and properly dried.

2. Measure out a small dose: Using a precise scale, measure out a sub-perceptual dose of dried mushroom, usually between 0.1-0.5 grams.

3. Decide on a dosing schedule: Some people microdose every three days, while others microdose daily for a week and then take a break for several days.

4. Consume the mushrooms: Either eat the dried mushrooms whole or grind them into a powder and mix them into food or a beverage. It's important to be consistent with the method of consumption.

5. Observe the effects: Take note of any subtle changes in mood, creativity, energy levels, or overall wellbeing. Keep a journal to track any noticeable effects.

6. Adjust the dose if needed: If you don't feel any effects after a few days of micro-dosing, you can gradually increase the dose by 0.1-0.2 grams. However, it's important to avoid taking a dose that is high enough to cause a noticeable psychedelic experience.

It's important to note that micro-dosing psilocybin mushrooms is a relatively new practice, and there is still limited scientific research on its effectiveness and potential risks. It's recommended to consult with a healthcare professional before starting a Micro dosing regimen. Additionally, psilocybin mushrooms are still illegal in many countries, so be sure to research the legal status in your area.

Chapter Twenty-One:

How to Prepare Medicinal Mushrooms

Medicinal mushrooms can be prepared in various ways depending on personal preference and the intended use. Here are some common methods:

1. Tea or decoction: This is one of the most popular ways to prepare medicinal mushrooms. To make tea, simply steep the mushroom in hot water for about 20 minutes. For a decoction, simmer the mushroom in water for 1-2 hours to extract more of the medicinal compounds. The resulting liquid can be consumed as is or mixed with other ingredients to improve the taste.

2. Tincture: A tincture is a concentrated extract made by soaking the mushroom in alcohol for several weeks to extract its medicinal compounds. The resulting liquid can be taken orally or added to food or drinks.

3. Powder: Dried mushrooms can be ground into a fine powder and added to food or drinks. This is a convenient way to consume medicinal mushrooms, especially if the taste or texture is unpleasant.

4. Capsules: Medicinal mushroom powders can be encapsulated for easy consumption. This is a good option for those who don't like the taste or texture of mushrooms.

5. Cooking: Many medicinal mushrooms can be added to soups, stews, and other dishes. They can be sautéed, roasted, or baked, depending on the recipe. Cooking mushrooms can help break down the tough cell walls and make their nutrients more bioavailable.

It's important to note that different mushroom species have different medicinal properties and require different preparation methods. It's best to consult a qualified healthcare practitioner or a mushroom expert for guidance on the proper preparation and use of specific medicinal mushrooms.

CHAPTER TWENTY-TWO:

Where Can I Sell Medicinal Mushrooms?

There are several options for selling medicinal mushrooms, depending on your location and business model. Here are a few possibilities:

1. Farmers' markets: Many farmers' markets allow vendors to sell mushrooms and other agricultural products. This can be a good option if you have a small operation and want to connect with local customers.

2. Online marketplaces: There are several online marketplaces that specialize in health food and supplements, such as Amazon, Etsy, and iHerb. You can list your products on these platforms and reach a wider audience.

3. Health food stores: Many health food stores carry medicinal mushrooms and other natural supplements. You can reach out to local stores and see if they are interested in carrying your products.

4. Direct-to-consumer sales: If you have a website or social media presence, you can sell directly to consumers. This can be a good option if you have a strong brand and want to build a loyal following.

5. Wholesale distribution: You can also sell your products to other businesses that specialize in natural supplements. This can be a good option if you have a large operation and want to scale your business.

Regardless of the option you choose, make sure to comply with any relevant regulations and certifications for selling medicinal mushrooms.

Printed in the USA
CPSIA information can be obtained
at www.ICGtesting.com
LVHW070324211023
761657LV00078B/1594

9 781916 707955